A Guide to Using the Anonymous Web in Libraries and Information Organizations

A Guide to Using the Anonymous Web in Libraries and Information Organizations provides practical guidance to those who are interested in integrating the anonymous web into their services. It will be particularly useful to those seeking to promote enhanced privacy for their patrons.

The book begins by explaining, in simple terms, what the anonymous web is, how it works, and its benefits for users. Lund and Beckstrom also explain why they believe access to the anonymous web should be provided in library and information organizations around the world. They describe how to provide access, as well as educate library users on how to utilize the anonymous web and navigate any challenges that might arise during implementation. The authors also encourage the development of library policies that guide appropriate conduct and filter content, where appropriate, in order to deter illegal activity.

A Guide to Using the Anonymous Web in Libraries and Information Organizations reminds us that libraries and other information providers have a duty to educate and support their communities, while also preserving privacy. Demonstrating that the anonymous web can help them to fulfil these obligations, this book will be essential reading for library and information professionals working around the world.

Brady D. Lund is a PhD candidate at Emporia State University's School of Library and Information Management (Emporia, KS, USA), where he also earned his Master of Library Science degree. His research focuses on scholarly communications, information technology in libraries, information and data ethics, and data science.

Matthew A. Beckstrom has been with the Lewis & Clark Library in Helena Montana since 1999 as the Systems Manager/Librarian. He received his undergraduate degree in computer science from Montana State University Billings in 2010, and graduated with his Masters of Information Science in Information Systems degree, with two graduate academic certificates from the University of North Texas in 2012. He is currently on the Montana Library Association board as the chapter councilor for the American Library Association, is the chair of the Montana Intellectual Freedom Committee, and serves on the American Library Association Council.

Routledge Guides to Practice in Libraries, Archives and Information Science

This series provides essential practical guides for those working in libraries, archives, and a variety of other information science professions around the globe.

Including authored and edited volumes, the series will help to enhance practitioners' and students' professional knowledge and will also encourage sharing of best practices between different countries, as well as between different types and sizes of organisations.

Titles published in the series include:

Guidance for Librarians Transitioning to a New Environment
Tina Herman Buck and Sara Duff

Recordkeeping in International Organizations
Archives in Transition in Digital, Networked Environments
Edited by Jens Boel and Eng Sengsavang

Trust and Records in an Open Digital Environment
Edited by Hrvoje Stančić

Assessment as Information Practice
Evaluating Collections and Services
Edited by Gaby Haddow and Hollie White

A Guide to Using the Anonymous Web in Libraries and Information Organizations
Enhancing Patron Privacy and Information Access
Brady D. Lund and Matthew A. Beckstrom

For more information about this series, please visit: https://www.routledge.com/ Routledge-Guides-to-Practice-in-Libraries-Archives-and-Information-Science/ book-series/RGPLAIS

A Guide to Using the Anonymous Web in Libraries and Information Organizations

Enhancing Patron Privacy and Information Access

Brady D. Lund and Matthew A. Beckstrom

Routledge
Taylor & Francis Group

LONDON AND NEW YORK

Cover image: © Vertigo3d / Getty Images

First published 2022
by Routledge
4 Park Square, Milton Park, Abingdon, Oxon OX14 4RN

and by Routledge
605 Third Avenue, New York, NY 10158

Routledge is an imprint of the Taylor & Francis Group, an informa business

British Library Cataloguing-in-Publication Data
A catalogue record for this book is available from the British Library

Library of Congress Cataloging-in-Publication Data
A catalog record has been requested for this book

ISBN: 978-0-367-55476-7 (hbk)
ISBN: 978-0-367-54945-9 (pbk)
ISBN: 978-1-003-09373-2 (ebk)

DOI: 10.4324/9781003093732

Typeset in Times NR MT Pro
by KnowledgeWorks Global Ltd.

Contents

List of Figures   vi
List of Tables   vii
Acknowledgement   viii

Introduction: The Anonymous Web and Libraries   1

1 History of the Internet and Introduction
  to the Anonymous Web   7

2 What Is the Anonymous Web?   21

3 History of Internet Privacy and Libraries   38

4 Tor around the World   50

5 Integrating the Anonymous Web in Libraries
  and Information Organizations   70

6 Anonymous Web Education   83

7 A Role for Library and Information Science Researchers
  in Anonymous Web Research   99

8 Case Examples of Anonymous Web Adoption
  in Information Organizations   110

9 Conclusion: What Have We Learned? What Can We Do?   116

The Big Glossary of the Anonymous Web and Related Topics   120
Major Websites on the Anonymous Web   128
Index   135

Figures

1.1   Iceberg Analogy for the Relationship among Surface, Deep, and Dark WEb   8
1.2   Example of Data Communication   14
2.1   Tor Browser Home Screen   29
2.2   Example of Message Encryption Within the Tor Network   30
3.1   Timeline of General Computer Technology and Library Technology Developments   39
4.1   Countries That Attempt to Restrict Access to Tor   51
4.2   Five Countries with Most Tor Users   64
4.3   Four Countries with the Most Tor Bridge Users   65
4.4   Tor Bridges: A Map of Censorship Activity   67
5.1   Tor Project Download Interface   72
5.2   The Onion Service   74
6.1   Learner Feedback Following Presentations With and Without Analogy   91
7.1   Keyword Co-occurrence Visualization for Tor Studies   107

Tables

1.1   Term frequencies in article titles for each search term   10

1.2   Term frequencies in article keywords for each search term   10

Acknowledgment

We would like to acknowledge the support of our editor and publisher for this work of ours. We also want to acknowledge and the efforts of fighters for privacy, freedom, and equity worldwide. It is your work that has inspired ours.

Introduction

The Anonymous Web and Libraries

Greetings, Reader! Welcome to our discussion of the anonymous web and libraries. In this book, we will provide a thorough background on the history of the anonymous web, describe how it works, how it is distinct from other privacy/anonymity platforms, address some ethical issues, and discuss how it has and can be used in libraries.

You may have happened upon this volume after reading our previous book on the "Dark web" and wondered "what is the difference?" For the majority of the content of this book, the distinctions are dramatic. Our prior book was intended as a general read on the topic of the anonymous web, geared to a non-library and information science audience. I am sure that, if you read it, you learned some things that were relevant to your work as a librarian, but this was not the central aim. We were much more interested in informing the average consumer about risks to Internet privacy and ways to avoid censorship.

In this book, on the other hand, the LIS professional is the intended audience. We wanted to write a book (which might complement our earlier one) that discusses topics like "how do I go about making my library a Tor relay?" and "how can I teach my library's patrons about how anonymous web technology works?" We also wanted a forum to speculate about how universities could offer courses and/or coursework related to the infrastructure and benefits of the anonymous web – and not just discussion of how the platform has been used for criminal activity (which exists in some universities' criminal justice departments). We wanted to discuss the platform's relevance to LIS professionals and researchers in a way that is technical – but not too dense as to scare the more casual reader away.

Why Should We Care About the Anonymous Web?

We are glad that you asked! We would never use scare tactics to sell books, so trust us when we say that web democracy and freedom is under attack! Take a look at the Internet Archive's new (as of October 2021) Wayforward Machine (https://wayforward.archive.org/) if you want to see their own projection of what the Internet may look like in only 25 years. We are talking

DOI: 10.4324/9781003093732-1

about an Internet where there is no freedom to set up a new web venture – to become the next Mark Zuckerberg or Jeff Bezos (our personal thoughts on those two aside, they were self-made billionaires) – because the sites to which users have access are strictly controlled by an oversight panel that supports monopolies and controls social dialogue. To a reader in the Global North – developed countries like the United States and United Kingdom – that may seem a bit far-fetched, but it exists right now in certain parts of the world, like China and Iran. In China, for instance, social media from other countries is blocked, while giant social media monopolies WeChat and Sina Weibo (which are designed to allow the government to monitor citizens' activities) are the only platforms available. By the way, even Facebook itself is not that far off from one of these Internet monopolies. They are widely known for buying up competitors to retain a monopoly, on invading upon the privacy of users, and for improperly monitoring for deliberate misinformation shared on the site (including by political figures).

In other situations, political dissidents, journalists, and whistleblowers all over the world are constantly fighting to get their words out. Imagine being a free thinker in a country like Iran where your government is trying to prevent anyone from expressing their views and stopping them from posting their experiences on the Internet. In the Human Rights Watch World Report 2021 (https://www.hrw.org/world-report/2021), they detail the Iranian attempts in 2019 to shut down dissident protests using excessive, sometimes lethal force, and of course, restricting access to the Internet. The Freedom of the Press Foundation is a great source of information on how journalists around the world use the anonymous web to stay in contact with dissidents and whistleblowers (https://freedom.press/organizations/tor-project/). Many Non-Governmental Organizations that do business in foreign countries, will have their employees use the anonymous web to protect their communications.

As librarians and information professionals, we have a duty to preserve the basic human rights of our patrons and every human, including the right to intellectual freedom and privacy. It is written right into the Code of Ethics of the American Library Association (ALA, 2021), the Chartered Institute of Library and Information Professionals (UK) (CILIP, 2021), and the International Federation of Library Associations (IFLA, 2021). Further, we must consider what rights we value as INDIVIDUALS, because there are many cases where if libraries are not the ones to protect rights, then nobody and nothing will. Think of how libraries welcome all populations everyone, including the poor, homeless, mentally and physically ill, ex-criminals, refugees, young children, and 100 year olds. Libraries do not care where you were born, what color your skin is, or what you believe in. What other places do that? Increasingly, few places offer refuge to any of these populations and, without libraries, they would be left without any place to go for shelter, comfort, to expand their knowledge and participate in society. We should think of all human rights, including the rights to online freedom and privacy, with the same urgency and call to duty as we do for the protection of vulnerable populations. If privacy is valuable to us as individuals, then we must make sure it is valuable to our libraries, because they may become the final bastion of hope in a world of ever-increasing intrusions. Any other organization or service that can be influenced by outside money (including politics) is vulnerable when the data being collected is potentially worth billions of dollars.

The anonymous web is a needed, necessary, and key part of the solution to this issue. It can ensure web users' privacy and security while circumventing censorship and providing information access. It cannot be the only solution – we must also support non-profit web organizations that fight for online privacy rights like the Electronic Frontier Foundation and Wikipedia – but it is perhaps the best solution to ensure personal rights of web users when using the Internet today. It is also the source of some significant controversy, owing, in no small part, to its immense power. Without regular use and support for the network, actors who aim to shut down the network can gain greater footing. Libraries, and applications and users of the anonymous web should forge a symbiotic relationship where the libraries provide support and infrastructure for anonymous web applications and users, networks and anonymous web networks they in return provide tools to help libraries fulfill their obligations to preserve the intellectual freedom and privacy of patrons for everyone. How does this book fit into this relationship? Well, it tells you how to get it done.

Writing Style

There is no point in writing a book if you cannot have fun with it. So, do not expect this book to be a dry, scholarly text. It is scholarly, in the sense that it is well-researched, but not in the sense that we are going to do everything, as authors, to make this book utterly painful for you to read. We get no joy showing that we are the smartest people in the room (we already know it!). There are no hidden meanings that need to be scrutinized (or are there?). We write as we like to read – that is, well-informed, but conversational and often (hopefully) humorous. We have been criticized for overusing parentheses (if you have not already noticed yourself), but that is an intentional choice. If we understand that all of our interactions are governed by unquestioned practices, then our use of the World Wide Web is one of the most egregious acts of unquestioning. Even with knowledge of the threats the Internet poses to users, we continue to engage in the same web use behaviors. We also continue to criticize book authors for using parentheses too much – well that stops now (of course, many of you would not have noticed the parentheses had we not brought it up and now will not be able to ignore it).

You may also note a fair number of popular culture references throughout the book. Maybe it is the two decades I (Brady) have spent hammering Eminem, Outkast, and Kendrick Lamar through my headphones, but dropping references is one of my favorite things to do while writing (and, I think, helpful to the reader). Of course, pop culture references can be a bit more tricking when writing a book intended for a global audience. My knowledge of the National Football League is probably not particularly relevant to a reader from South Africa – but hey, pull Wikipedia up on your device and maybe you will learn something new. It is also possible that the references will go right over your head, in which case you will be none the wiser!

The Organization of This Book

Lund and Beckstrom are no Deleuze and Guattari, so if you are looking for a fresh take on the organization of a book, well… sorry to disappoint. This book will have a traditional, linear structure, but we will try to throw in a few surprises to keep you engaged.

Chapter 1 provides an introduction to the anonymous web and historical context in the history of the Internet and privacy technology. The focus of this historical overview will be on how evolution of the Internet paved the way for anonymous web platforms like Tor.

Chapter 2 will discuss and show the way that several of the most popular anonymous web services work and how they evolved to offer anonymous services. We will discuss the Tor platform, the I2P platform, and the Freenet platform.

Discussed in Chapter 3 is the relationship between libraries and Internet privacy and the anonymous web. Libraries have always been a source of information for their users. That information has varied throughout history to include books that cover almost any topic, programming or events that inspire, entertain, or educate, and access to the Internet. Depending on national or local laws, libraries' ability to offer access to Internet resources changes. Some libraries can be open with access to the Internet and offer their patrons full access to the visible and hidden Internet. Some libraries must be more careful based on filtering requirements.

Even though the Internet is worldwide and the anonymous web rides along with it, it is not equally available everywhere. Chapter 4 will discuss the implementation of the anonymous web in different parts of the world. We will discuss North America, Europe, Asia, and Australian regions. Each section will include a basic understanding of the current laws regarding access to the Internet and the anonymous web. Keep in mind that we are librarians, not lawyers, so our research will be our best advice given the information we can gather, but is not in any way legal advice. We will show how libraries are currently using the Internet and the anonymous web.

Chapter 5 will discuss how the anonymous web can actually be implemented in libraries. Turning on the anonymous web is not as simple as just flipping a switch. In many cases, it will require some planning. There are a lot of factors to consider. First, which anonymous web platforms do you want to implement? There are many, many types beyond the three we discuss in the book. Each one has their strengths and weaknesses. Each one has benefits and disadvantages based on how they will be used. Understanding of what the patrons want or need is vital. Once you decide on a platform or two to implement, how do you do it? Once again, plan is needed. What additional infrastructure is required? How will this affect my regular Internet and other online resources? How much will it cost? This chapter will be a great guide to get started. Obviously, each library and every region will have wildly different requirements and needs, but this will be a start.

Chapter 6 will discuss how libraries may educate patrons about the anonymous web. You have turned on the anonymous web in your library. Your patrons can happily use the Internet more safely and securely. Great. Now what? The next step is helping them to use it. An education plan is vital to making it successful. Starting with simple guides to get people started, to full one-day demonstrational classes will be covered. Even though the anonymous web provides easy access to a more secure and private web, it still requires some careful practices that help to maintain that security. Users must change their behavior when on the anonymous web. They have to be careful where they tread, and they have to always be thinking about what they are doing. Larger educational classes can cover more information on how the Internet and the anonymous web work, and how to make it work for even the most casual browser.

Chapter 7 discusses the need to expand research on the anonymous web from a library and information science perspective. Most of the research existing today takes a hard science/information systems perspective. There is a clear need to increase research from a social science/human-centered perspective in order to expand the legitimacy of these platforms.

Chapter 8 will provide several short example cases of how the anonymous web may be implemented in a variety of library and information organization settings. These examples will give you a good idea of how we would approach implementing the anonymous web and educating patrons about it based on different library types, situations, and nations around the world.

Finally, Chapter 9 will serve as a wrap-up. The Internet is a growing, evolving space that changes and adapts based on current trends and needs. The anonymous web, as a subset of the evolving Internet, must also adapt and change with it. Libraries must continue to stay up to date on the anonymous web, its changes, and new technology. In this chapter, we will discuss how libraries can stay up to date on the anonymous web, how it changes, and how to keep up with it.

At the very end of the book, we include a glossary of key terms related to the anonymous web and an extensive index of websites available on the anonymous web (and a few words of advice on navigating the anonymous web).

Let Us Begin

We appreciate that you have selected our book to satisfy all of your anonymous web-related information needs. Be assured that this work is the product of nearly five years of research and discussion about the anonymous web, and direct experiences by the authors. We doubt you will find a more extensive and practical book out there. So, put on your favorite sweater, slip into a comfy chair, and dig into *A Guide to Using the Anonymous Web in Libraries and Information Organizations.*

References

American Library Association (ALA). (2021, October 7). *Professional ethics.* Retrieved from https://www.ala.org/tools/ethics

Chartered Institute of Library and Information Professionals (CILIP). (2021, October 7). *Code of professional practice for library and information professionals.* Retrieved from https://cdn.ymaws.com/www.cilip.org.uk/resource/collection/ B29DAF42-6319-406F-8985-52CF355B98D7/code_of_professional_practice_ for_library_and_.pdf

International Federation of Library Associations (IFLA). (2021, October 7). *IFLA code of ethics for librarians and other information workers.* Retrieved from https:// www.ifla.org/wp-content/uploads/2019/05/assets/faife/publications/IFLA%20 Code%20of%20Ethics%20-%20Long_0.pdf

1 History of the Internet and Introduction to the Anonymous Web

As libraries become increasingly system-oriented in their resources and services, an assurance of privacy is requisite. Yet, this is an assurance that most libraries cannot honestly offer. Even though privacy is a core value of librarianship (American Library Association, 2019), many libraries are lacking in this area. A huge part of this challenge is due to the ambiguity about what "privacy" really means, how individuals' privacy is lost, and what strategies should be taken to defend it. Society already asks librarians to know so much about so many different things, and intimate knowledge of computer security and information systems concepts and theory is often complex enough to comprise entire masters-level programs.

Another issue is the complexity of systems available to libraries. Most of the time, libraries and librarians are trying to "keep up" with the latest trends or new services that are offered. Library users come into the library without thinking about privacy, they just want to get the latest best seller or access the Internet (Kim and Noh, 2014). It has become the role and, in some cases, the duty of libraries to protect their users' privacy (Witt, 2017). Virtually every state in the United States, most provinces in Canada, and many nations and municipalities in Europe have some kind of law that dictates how privacy should be treated within libraries, with each law/policy being somewhat distinct (Ayala, 2018; American Library Association, 2021).

What we offer in this book, then, is not a comprehensive guide to all facets of information privacy (as established, that seems like too much to fit in one book and too much to ask of a busy professional to digest in any meaningful way to their professional duties). Instead, we highlight one class of technologies that, while not a "cure all" by any means, is relatively simple to implement and use – it does not require any programming knowledge to install or utilize – and provides a level of security that should leave most users confident in the privacy of their web data.

What Is the Anonymous Web (From 30,000 Feet)?

The most prominent visual aid used to describe the relationship of the surface, deep, and dark web is the iceberg analogy (Beckstrom and Lund, 2019). In this analogy, as shown in Figure 1.1, one is asked to envision an

DOI: 10.4324/9781003093732-2

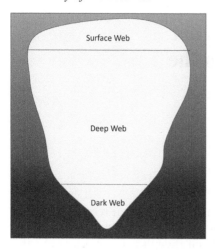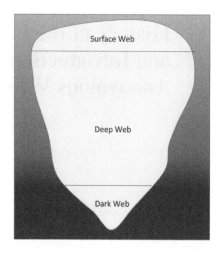

Figure 1.1 Iceberg Analogy for the Relationship among Surface, Deep, and Dark Web

iceberg floating in the ocean, where only about 10% of the iceberg is visible above water while the remaining 90% is hidden below the water's surface (but is nonetheless fundamental to the stabilization of the entire structure). Similarly, only about 10% of content on Internet networks is freely available to anyone who wishes to access it. The remaining 90% of the content is part of the deep web. The term "deep" or "hidden" web comes from the iceberg terminology above. It is the content that is not visible "to the naked eye," but is nonetheless crucial to the operation of the Internet.

Specifically, the deep web consists of the content that a user must have some special authorization or software to access. This does not (necessarily) mean content that you need some government clearance to access; the deep web includes all content that is password protected (He et al., 2007). Your Facebook account, Netflix videos, and library system content are all part of the deep web. Think back to our iceberg – you can readily access the part of the iceberg above the water, but you would need to have some sort of additional equipment to get to the part of the iceberg under the water. For example, you would need a snorkel or a diving suit. With the deep web, you would use simple tools like passwords or special software. It is not nearly as ominous as the term "deep web" makes it seem. Nonetheless, the deep web is incredibly important. Imagine if there was no way to hide content – if everything you put on there was freely available to everyone and could be modified by anyone. Companies would lose profit motive to produce new content, users would not feel that their content is secure. It would be a virtual free-for-all, with a lack of accountability for users. It would *not* be the web we know today. So, while the deep web is not as complex and ominous as you might have hoped, it is nonetheless absolutely critical that it exist as a part of our regular Internet access, and that we understand how it is accessed.

So, what is the anonymous web? The anonymous web is a subset of deep web content that is available only by connecting to a special network that lies over or around the "normal" Internet. The anonymous web is essentially a hitchhiker that uses the Internet's infrastructure but adds extra layers of encryption that require special software in order to access content. This "special software" is generally a web browser designed to support an anonymous web platform. The Onion Router (Tor), the most popular anonymous web platform, uses a modified version of the Firefox browser. Looking at our iceberg once again, think of the anonymous web an integrated (internal) part of the ice. It is there, but you cannot see it unless you are able to "tunnel" into the ice and get to it. Anonymous web software was originally developed by the U.S. military as a means for secure communications between whistleblowers, various foreign agencies, and military officials from around the globe (Syverson, Goldschlag, and Reed, 1997). The anonymous web provides advanced privacy and security to users (why we believe it is important as the topic of this book).

The enhanced privacy/security of the anonymous web is also what has led to its scrutiny by researchers and law enforcement (Chen, 2011). Because the anonymous web severely limits the ability to track or identify users, it is susceptible to use for criminal exchanges of information, weapons, drugs, etc. However, we would argue that misuse by a relatively small proportion of users should not warrant shutting down the platform. The use of the anonymous web for legal and important reasons outweighs the illegal use concerns. This does not just include the average library user browsing the Internet but journalists abroad, freedom fighters, whistleblowers, etc. When the Internet originally became publicly available, it was also a breeding ground for illegal activity. That may be perceived as an ad hominem attack against Internet users who reject the anonymous web, but it is really intended to suggest that some aspects of the anonymous web are problematic, as presently constituted, but have considerable potential for being adopted for legitimate uses. This does require people to be willing to use the platform – to trust us when we say there are no risks to using the anonymous web as long as you do so lawfully (just like this is not problem in using a car or the Internet if you do so legally).

Is It Legal to Use the Anonymous Web?

For most Internet users, it is legal to access the anonymous web, so long as you are not engaging in illegal activities. This is particularly true for readers in the United States, Canada, and Western Europe, where few, if any, restrictions exist. However, a few jurisdictions may have different rules – particularly nations that are not quite friendly to individual information privacy. Chapter 4 of this book will dig deep, country-by-country, into policies regarding the use of the anonymous web.

Why "Anonymous Web"

To demonstrate why we selected the term "Anonymous Web" for the focus of this book, and also set out a topic map for what we will be discussing throughout this book, we performed a word frequency analysis of titles and keywords for "dark web," "Tor," and "anonymous web," three terms commonly used to describe the central topic that this book will cover. Table 1.1 provides a comparison of the ten most frequency substantive terms (not "a," "an," and "the") in article titles by search term, while Table 1.2 does the same for article keywords.

Based on this table, it should be evident why we would want to avoid the term "dark web" – it has simply become too intertwined with illegal activity, while our goal with this book is to do the very opposite of encouraging

Table 1.1 Term frequencies in article titles for each search term

"Dark Web"	Freq.	"Tor"	Freq.	"Anonymous Web"	Freq.
Web	16	Tor	20	Anonymous	11
Dark	16	Network	5	Web	7
Narcotics	3	Browsing	3	Internet	5
Deep	3	Onion	3	Anonymity	4
Laundering	2	Anonymity	3	Privacy	3
Trafficking	2	Pi	2	Free	2
Million	2	Privacy	2	Browsing	2
Darknet	2	Routing	2	Preserving	2
Study	2	OnionDNS	2	Networks	2
Hacker	2	Classification	2	Probabilities	2

Table 1.2 Term frequencies in article keywords for each search term

"Dark Web"	Freq.	"Tor"	Freq.	"Anonymous Web"	Freq.
Darknets	7	Data encryption	5	Anonymity	6
Cybercriminals	5	Open-source software	3	Privacy	5
Computer crimes	4	Routing	3	Internet	4
Money laundering	4	Anonymity	3	Websites	3
Invisible web	3	Censorship	3	Computer security	3
Terrorism	3	Computer networks	3	Web browsing	2
Web search engines	2	Network routing protocols	2	Tor	2
Internet ethics	2	Browsers	2	Internet security	2
Silk road	2	Http	2	Computer network resources	2
Cryptomarkets	2	Privacy	2	Access to information	2

illegal activities. When readers see "dark web," they expect stories of criminal escapades and are disappointed if that's not what they get. Starting out the name of a tool with the word dark immediately puts the thought into negative. Starting a tool with the word anonymous has a different effect. It implies privacy and security. As one of the Amazon reviewers of our 2019 book, Casting Light on the Dark Web, opined, "if you are planning on doing something illegal using the dark web and hope not to get caught, this book is probably insufficient." Of course, helping people conduct illegal activity without getting caught was not the goal with that book, or this book, at all. So, "dark web" is straight-out.

"Tor" has worked hard to ensure its name is associated with decency rather than dark web activities. There are several reasons, however, that we elected not to use it in our title. First, and most importantly, Tor is only one of many anonymous web platforms; we want to be inclusive of all means in which to access the anonymous web, not show preference for one particular platform based on its popularity. Additionally, writing an entire book solely on Tor seems inappropriate, as neither of us authors are affiliated with Tor nor the work they do, and we do not want our work to be perceived as being explicitly supported by, or supportive of, the Tor Project. Finally, "Tor" is just not a super-appealing term to include in a book title (would you have picked up this book if a "Guide to Tor in libraries" was the title?). So, while Tor has a prominent position in this book, it was not appropriate for the title of this book.

"Anonymous Web" balances technical, theoretical, and practical concepts. It conveys, essentially, the same ideas as "Tor" for people who are familiar with both terms but is broader (encompasses all platforms, rather than just a single one). Keywords were not the only (probably not even the biggest) reason why we selected anonymous web for the title of this book, but the comparison of this term to "dark web" demonstrates why we would want to avoid the latter, based on our desire for this book to reach library practitioners genuinely interested in promoting privacy rather than just people looking for some interesting stories. That said, we are proud of the work we did in *Casting Light on the Dark Web* and encourage you to consider it as a companion to this book.

A Brief History of the Internet and the Anonymous Web

Mathematical Theory and the Birth of the "Computer"

Modern computing technology and networks is only viable because of centuries of theoretical development. The purpose of this book is not to exhaust you with history and theory; however, we believe it is appropriate to at least touch on these topics as a way to introduce what the anonymous web is and how it works. There has been a critique of "great man" histories for many decades – with the crux of this argument being that important developments are the product of time and culture, not one genius. We acknowledge this fact but are nonetheless going to focus a bit on important historical figures, if nothing else, because that is the learning style with which the typical modern learner is accustomed. Furthermore, we are going to be a bit selective in our history, since this is, after all, not intended to be a history book. So, please use this history as a jumping-off point for further study.

First, an important definition. A *computer* is "one that computes." It does not necessarily mean, as it is colloquially referred to as today, an electronic technology. In fact, manual "computers" existed for centuries before the advent of electronic technology (Grier, 2013). Before computation could be automated, people were employed to compute data (at which time, "computer" was a job title, like "teacher" or "farmer"). The computers we think of today are a much more recent development.

Boolean algebra, introduced by 19th-century British mathematician George Boole, was a fundamental development for the trajectory of the modern electronic computer (Jukna, 2012). In Boolean algebra, the digits of "0" and "1" are used to represent the values of "false" and "true." With this notation, information can be communicated in a simplistic form that can be compressed and also be interpreted by an electrical circuit (as "off" and "on"). For a computer, each piece of information (0 or 1) is called a bit. A "byte" consists of eight bits (/switches/signals) and is the basic building block of computing systems, like the cell for a living creature. For instance, one byte is used to store value of a single letter (A–Z) – this is represented by binary code, such as "01000001" for "a." Modern computers have the capacity to store huge amounts of this data. It is not unsurprising to see a modern laptop computer hold 4 gigabytes (4 billion bytes or 32 billion bits) of Random Access Memory (RAM), or working memory that can be utilized while the computer is operating, and 128 gigabytes (128 billion bytes or 1.024 trillion bits) of storage in the solid-state drive (SSD), or permanent memory that is stored even when the computer is not in operation (like all your programs and files). To put this storage capacity in context, War and Peace is nearly 600,000 words in length; averaging four letters per word, we are talking about 2.4 million characters. This means the RAM on your laptop is capable of storing more data than 1600 copies of War and Peace just within its working memory. As another example, this chapter, save on our computers, has a file size of 23 kilobytes (23,000 bytes). How many characters (letters and spaces) do you think it contains? If you said 23,000 bytes, you would be correct.

Alan Turing, another British mathematician, contributed what might be considered the first true electronic computer. The "Turing Machine," unlike modern computers that utilize RAM, utilized a strip of magnetized tape upon which symbols (bits of data) were printed that could communicate to the "computer" (through the attention or exacerbation of electrical current by the tape) what actions to take (Turing and Copeland, 2004). The primary difference between the Turing tape and modern computer memory is that the Turing tape functioned in a linear manner (the tape can only be read in order), while RAM, as indicated by the name (random access), can be accessed in any order, allowing for variability and more complex computing operations. Regardless, Turing was one of the first to take Boole's principles and apply them to a storage device that could be read by a computer.

In the second-half of the 20th century, there was no figure more important for the communication of electrical data than Claude Shannon. Earlier, when reading about how 8 bits comprise 1 byte, you may have wondered "why 8?" Why not, for instance, 10, which would work well with multiples of 10 used in the metric system? Shannon introduced the concept of information entropy, or uncertainty, which suggests that, when information is communicated in a channel, there is a chance that it will be distorted (Shannon, 1948). For example, we might send the message 010101, but problems with the channel's quality, such as the cable that connects two servers, may flip one of those 0s so that the message reads 110101. This flipping could, and historically did, cause significant challenges to communicating message via a network. To account for distortion, most computer data is highly redundant. If there are two states for each bit of data (0 and 1), then only five bits ($2^5 = 32$) are needed to encode every letter, and seven bits ($2^7 = 128$) are needed to encode every symbol on your keyboard. The final bits are redundant pieces of data, used when a distortion has occurred to help the computer identify the correct symbol.

In many cases, data uncertainty (will the next bit be a 0 or a 1) can be reduced using algorithms, such that eight bits is not necessary. The reduction of redundancy/uncertainty can be used to compress a message/file, such that it is more efficient to store and send. Compression is invaluable in taking a large package of data (like an entire software program that you download) and communicate/download it over a reasonable period of time.

How Networking Works

We are not electrical engineers, but if you are interested in knowing, at a bit more granular level, how networking works (like, how whole messages can be sent using bunches of electrical wires), we can offer a brief introduction. Perhaps the easiest way to describe it is by looking at an example of how an Ethernet cable works. Ethernet cables are those long cables with the connectors at the end that look like a large rectangle with a smaller clip-like rectangle on top of it. They look very similar to a phone cable (because they are) but are larger and contain more wires (because they generally carry a lot more data).

Your Ethernet cables consist of eight copper wires, grouped in pairs and intertwined together, and protected within a cable "jacket" (the part on the exterior of the cable that keeps the wires from being exposed to the external world). Each wire ends in connector pins, which are what passes the communications to and from the cable. Signals begin to be passed

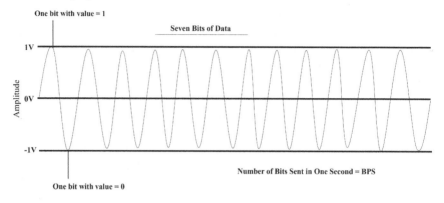

Figure 1.2 Example of Data Communication

to the cable wires through a device's network interface card, or network interface controller (NIC). The NIC is connected or built into the computer's motherboard and transfers data into signals. In each cable, there are certain wires that are to transmit signals and others that receive signals (except for more recent, higher speed networks, which use all eight wires simultaneously).

Figure 1.2 is a visual representation of the flow of current through the wires. The current has an amplitude, measured in volts (V), which is the amount of power in a signal at a point in time (think of an electric guitars amplifier or "amp"). Voltage is used to communicate data. Sensors that convert the electrical current measure shifts in voltage at fixed intervals in time. Depending on the amount of voltage, a value can be assigned in the form of the binary 0 or 1. So, the wire may, at one point, transfer a voltage of –1 V, which is interpreted as the value of 0, and then transfer a voltage of 1 V at the next measured interval, which is interpreted as 1. In this way, electrical current can be converted into data which, as we already know from earlier, is how the computer operates and creates everything wonderful with which we interact.

The amount of data that can be communicated on the wire in a given amount of time is measured using bits per second (bps) (Metcalfe and Boggs, 1976). Most computers operate on 10 MBPS (10 million bits per second), 100 MBPS (100 million bits per second), or 1 GBPS (1 billion bits per second). This means that the voltage is being measured tens of millions, hundreds of millions, or even billons of times per second. This is how it is possible for a system that consists only of changing amounts of electrical power to create something like an entire, streaming Netflix video. This is also why, as we will discuss later in this book, the anonymous web is much slower. The amount of encryption and network configuration involved in the network significantly slows how fast the correct signals can be transmitted to your computer.

If you have ever wondered why your AM radio signal goes fuzzy when you drive under telephone lines, this understanding of networking should give you a good idea. Phone signals travel very similarly to Internet signals, just at different frequencies. AM is short for "amplitude modulated" radio, where signals are transmitted through the medium of the air (as opposed to through the medium of a wire), which is composed of particles that vibrate to different frequencies, and different radio signals are sent by changing the amplitude of a carrier signal, essentially a baseline signal that the actual signal (the radio program that you are listening to) rides along (Roder, 1931). AM signals travel at very low frequencies (~500–1600 KHz – kilohertz, or thousand hertz), compared to frequency modulated (FM) signals that travel between 88 and 108 megahertz (million hertz). The low frequency and amplitude ranges of an AM signal make it very susceptible to interference, or noise, which is why the signal is generally much poorer than an FM signal and can be impacted by interference from other electrical signals, like those sent along the telephone lines. The benefit of these signals is that they travel very well through a variety of media (like air, trees, hills), which means the signal can extend farther (which is why I can listen to sports radio from Kansas City in Wichita – 200 miles away – on AM signals, but cannot pick up an FM signal from 30 miles away at times). These principles of radio signals are also what makes wireless Internet possible, with communications between your Wi-Fi modem and wireless NIC.

In order to get from these basic concepts of networking to a massive network of interconnected systems like the Internet, a significant upscaling had to occur. Data must pass through intermediaries along the way, like your Internet Service Provider, who collect the signals from the servers of the website with which you are wanting to connect and then routes the signal to your Internet protocol (IP) Address, where it arrives at your house, is converted from an analog to a digital signal (continuous to noncontinuous shifts in voltage) and is transferred to your device.

The Foundations of the Internet

The "Internet," as we know it today, was preceded by a United States' military project named Advanced Research Projects Agency Network (ARPANET), which at its height connected several government agencies and dozens of higher education institutions, primarily on the coasts of the United States (Abbate, 1994). The technology behind ARPANET was revolutionary for telecommunications. "Traditional" communication systems required a telephone operator to literally connect calls (circuit switching), essentially serving the role of what the Internet Service Provider does in the networking example above. ARPANET, however, utilized *packet switching*, where a packet of data tells the network from where and to where the communication should be sent, allowing the message to be directed automatically to where it needed to be (McQuillan, Richer, and Rosen, 1980). This allowed for a single permanent infrastructure to be used to communicate data (without this development, we might have to have an Internet operator connect us with the website we want to visit).

By the mid-1980s, dozens of networks were developed using the concepts developed with ARPANET (Lukasik, 2010). ARPANET itself had evolved into a couple of robust networks for military and research communications. Each network "did its own thing," so to speak – they were designed for a single specific purpose. However, a movement to create a single network that bridged all of these smaller networks was gaining steam. The first commercial "Internet" providers, America On Line (AOL) and The World, emerged in the late 1980s; however, the data transferred by users with these early providers by no means matched the scale of what would develop only a few short years later.

In 1991, the World Wide Web (WWW), developed by Tim Berners-Lee, was released to the public. The WWW was fundamental to enabling the transfer of data over a unified Internet. Significantly, the WWW sets uniform standards for Internet resources (i.e., web pages that we view today) that enable them to be rendered in a readable format (in a web browser). Berners-Lee discussed how hypertext documents (essentially, webpages designed with HTML whose data is permanently stored on web servers) could be connected together (as in a web) and viewed through a computer interface (a web browser) (Berners-Lee et al., 1994). This system offers a stark contrast to the existing networks at the time, each of which had a specific purpose (like with ARPANET's focus on research and military), different procedures for formatting/sharing data, and lacked any permanence (data was shared contemporaneously, like with a phone call, rather than a true webpage).

Following the advent of the WWW, the basic Internet architecture we have today was put in place. Certainly, much of the minutiae has changed, from the emergence of search engines and social media to the interfaces of smart phones and other mobile devices, but the underlying concepts to get data from server A to device A to user A is remarkably stable. This stability has allowed plenty of time for threats to the WWW to emerge. As will be discussed throughout the remainder of this book, knowledge of how a system (in this case, the WWW) works informs strategies to tear it down or otherwise subvert it for personal or organizational gain. In response, organizations that support the Internet infrastructure must always be "one step ahead." Generally, being one step ahead means adding encryption in any case where data is being transferred from the user to a site's servers. However, there is a class of privacy/security developments that aim to improve on the actual design of the network itself (in other words, offer a "new and improved Internet"). This is the class that contains the "dark" or anonymous web. In the following chapter, we will discuss how exactly these anonymous web platforms offer alternatives to the communication system of the traditional web.

The Emergence of the Anonymous Web

Though various "dark" (dark in the sense that they cannot be accessed on the WWW) web platforms have emerged since the advent of the WWW, the first network of any considerable prominence to emerge was Tor. Tor was developed by the U.S. Department of Defense (as was ARPANET and the first modern computer – see a trend?) during the mid-1990s as a network to support secure communication between military outposts, political dissidents, spies, etc. (think of the specific use networks we discussed from the 1980s). It was the James Bond storyline that got away. Today, Tor (referred to only by its acronym today rather than the original full name) still serves this function; however, following its release to the public in 2002, Tor has also become a popular network for the general privacy seeker. As we will discuss in Chapter 2, Tor has become the most popular anonymous web platform for good reason: 1) It is well-designed and secure, 2) it is simple to use and offers the most flexibility to users, and 3) it still receives funding and support from the U.S. government. That is right: The "dark web" is a U.S. government-funded enterprise (so they must be highly supportive of its use by the public ... right?).

What Is *the Dark Web*?

We want to take this opportunity to make an important point of clarification: There is no single "dark web." It is not like the upside-down version of the Internet where everything is equal and opposite. Rather, "dark web" is used as a fairly generic term to refer to any network that 1) is not part of the "Internet" proper and/or 2) employs some network connection strategy that distorts or anonymizes user transactions. In other words, the "dark web" is "dark" because you cannot see it, not because it is evil. Furthermore, there is no single "web." It is instead many different webs. So again, this just goes to show why "dark web" is a poor name to use for this technology.

Other Anonymous Web Platforms

Following the release Tor, several other platforms emerged that gained some amount of prominence. Like Tor, these networks use unique routing strategies (that differ from the relatively straightforward nature of the WWW). The two additional anonymous web networks we discuss in this book – Freenet and I2P – were selected based on their relative popularity and because their method of routing traffic is sufficiently unique to demonstrate how different anonymous web networks can operate. Each of these two networks emerged around the beginning of the 21st century and are a bit more techy-oriented than the general-use, Firefox-lookalike, Tor.

Growing Pains

Anonymous web platforms have had their fair share of growing pains as they are adopted for public use. The whole "dark web" thing was not great for public relations. In fact, though we suggest conditions have improved now, the "dark web" has a pretty nasty history. At its peak, the Silk Road – a dark web marketplace that operated from 2011 to 2013 on Tor – did hundreds of millions of dollars in illegal exchanges during that period, with the biggest selling products being weapons and a host of illicit drugs (Van Hout and Bingham, 2013). Tor provided the platform and Bitcoin provided the form of exchange. Of course, this mark led to the romanticized media portrayals that persist today.

Most people who tell these stories about the Silk Road fail to mention that it was shut down by a joint FBI and Interpol raid in 2013. It turns out that Ross Williams "Dread Pirate Roberts" Ulbrecht, the site's developer and owner, did a little too much bragging about his "accomplishments" and may have let his true identity slip in a blog post that law enforcement was able to trace. Now the Dread Pirate is serving life in a U.S. high security prison in Tucson, AZ. Interestingly, Ulbrecht was actually arrested while visiting a branch of the San Francisco Public Library (The Guardian, 2013). So, the greatest impetus for the "dark web is evil" narrative is now seven years dead. In the meantime, the Tor network has worked fiercely to distance itself from the Silk Road and similar websites. We do not want to sugarcoat the anonymous web and act like incidents like that of the Silk Road did not happen, but we do want to emphasize that this use of Tor was not condoned by Tor, ended with the mastermind's arrest and has informed self-policing practices on Tor since that time in order to promote the sustainability of the network.

Blockchain, Bitcoin, and an Alternate History

Blockchain, and its use by cryptocurrencies, is a technology that, like the anonymous web, provides a high-level of anonymity (about who owns the currency and with whom it is exchanged). We mention it here because of its growing prominence and the potential promise it offers to enhance security offered by library and other information systems. Blockchain is also an interesting parallel story to the anonymous web because, although blockchain/cryptocurrency/Bitcoin was initially used almost exclusively to facilitate illegal activities on the "dark web," it has come to be recognized as a legitimate technology with applications for library and information organizations. Indeed, in early 2021, the overall market for cryptocurrencies boomed from one-half trillion to over two trillion dollars in value in a period of about three months (you can see the most recent values at coinmarketcap.com). Why has the anonymous web (and its underlying technology) not been given the same treatment (except from us two authors and a small handful of others)? Is it because credit card companies need a boogeyman in order to sell their worthless dark web scan products? Regardless, part of the purpose of this book is to flip that narrative about the anonymous web and bring to light its value, just as has been done for blockchain technology.

The Anonymous Web Today and Our Approach to Exploring It

Anonymous web platforms have learned from their past and this informs what they are doing now to support users. If you visit the homepage of Tor today (https://www.torproject.org), you will see that defense against tracking, surveillance, and censorship is highlighted, such that the site appears that it is advertising for any typical browser (just one that is super secure) – and they probably should, because to the typical user Tor may not be anything other than that. The older version of the site (https://web.archive.org/web/20110709171018/https://torproject.org/index.html.en) certainly did not say outright "people use this for illegal stuff," but it was much more open and honest about what the anonymous web is, that hidden services (onion sites) exist, and just generally that the network is not perfect. The modern site has erased virtually all mention of these facts. It does not really describe how the network works, does not mention. onion sites, and has removed most of its history section (and dissociated itself from any mention of "dark web"). That is one strategy – not one to which us authors subscribe, but nonetheless it is the route they have elected to take.

On the other end of this spectrum are media/researchers/marketers that are too stuck in 2013. These individuals are focused solely on how the dark/anonymous web can be used for illegal activity. This group may be waning in size, but it is seemingly growing in power. They have successfully made the vast majority of the general public scared about the "evil dark web" and even being associated with the topic. It is taboo. Because of that, it probably gave you a slight thrill just to pick up this book. We would argue that these perspectives – as you might imagine – are equally as inappropriate and harmful.

Our perspective in this book is to take a balanced approach, noting both the benefits and the pitfalls of the anonymous web. While we discuss how it can be used in libraries, we also caution that its implementation should be done with great care and in consultation with legal authorities (like a city or university attorney). It may not be feasible to provide unfettered access to anonymous web in your institution, you may need to develop policies that dictate when, how, and by whom this network can be used, but we will provide guidance that will support these decisions as well.

References

Abbate, J. E. (1994), *From ARPANET to Internet: A history of ARPA-sponsored computer networks, 1966–1988* (doctoral dissertation), University of Pennsylvania, Philadelphia, PA.

American Library Association. (2019, January 29), Library Bill of Rights, Retrieved from http://www.ala.org/advocacy/intfreedom/librarybill

American Library Association. (2021, April 22), State privacy laws regarding library records, Retrieved from https://ala.org/advocacy/privacy/statelaws

Ayala, D. (2018), "Shore to shore: How Europe's new data privacy laws help global libraries and patrons", *International Information & Library Review*, Vol. 50, No. 3, pp. 212–218.

Beckstrom, M. and Lund, B. D. (2019), *Casting light on the dark web: A guide for safe exploration*, Rowman and Littlefield, Lanham, MD.

Berners-Lee, T., Cailliau, R., Loutonen, A., Nielsen, H. F. and Secret, A. (1994), "The world-wide web", *Communications of the ACM*, Vol. 37, No. 8, pp. 76–82.

Chen, H. (2011), *Dark web: Exploring and data mining the dark side of the web*, Springer, New York, NY.

Grier, D. A. (2013), *When computers were human*, Princeton University Press, Princeton, NJ.

He, B., Patel, M., Zhang, Z. and Chen-Chuan, K. (2007), "Accessing the deep web", *Communications of the ACM*, Vol. 50, No. 5, pp. 94–101.

Jukna, S. (2012), *Boolean function complexity: Advances and frontiers*, Springer, London, UK.

Kim, D. S. and Noh, Y. (2014), "A study of public library patrons' understanding of library records and data privacy", *International Journal of Knowledge Content Development and Technology*, Vol. 4, No. 1, pp. 53–78.

Lukasik, S. (2010), "Why the ARPANET was built", *IEEE Annals of the History of Computing*, Vol. 33, No. 3, pp. 4–21.

McQuillan, J., Richer, I. and Rosen, E. (1980), "The new routing algorithm for the ARPANET", *IEEE Transactions on Communication*, Vol. 28, No. 5, pp. 711–719.

Metcalfe, R. M. and Boggs, D. R. (1976), "Ethernet: Distributed packet switching for local computer networks", *Communications of the ACM*, Vol. 19, No. 7, pp. 395–404.

Roder, H. (1931), "Amplitude, phase, and frequency modulation", *Proceedings of the Institute of Radio Engineers*, Vol. 19, No. 12, pp. 2145–2176.

Shannon, C. E. (1948), "A mathematical theory of communication", *The Bell System Technical Journal*, Vol. 27, No. 3, pp. 379–423.

Syverson, P. F., Goldschlag, D. M. and Reed, M. G. (1997), "Anonymous connections and onion routing", *IEEE Symposium on Security and Privacy*, Vol. 1997, pp. 44–54.

The Guardian (2013, November 21). *Silk Road founder Ross William Ulbrecht denied bail.* Retrieved from https://web.archive.org/web/201311220825571/http://www.theguardian.com/technology/2013/nov/21/silk-road-founder-held-without-bail

Turing, A. M. and Copeland, B. (2004), *The essential Turing*, Oxford University, Oxford, UK.

Van Hout, M. C. and Bingham, T. (2013), "Surfing the Silk Road: A study of users' experiences", *International Journal of Drug Policy*, Vol. 24, No. 6, pp. 524–529.

Witt, S. (2017), "The evolution of privacy within the American Library Association, 1906–2002", *Library Trends*, Vol. 65, No. 4, pp. 639–657.

2   What Is the Anonymous Web?

In this chapter, we discuss what makes the anonymous web unique. To do this, we return to our discussion of the Internet and networking from the prior chapter. By comparing the functioning of the Internet to that of the Tor network, the principles of what makes the anonymous web different and, most importantly, more secure, are revealed.

How the Internet Works

The Internet, at its most basic level, is nothing but a massive array of 1s and 0s (or you might say "yeses" and "nos"). These arrays of data, also called "packets," are organized to make meaning (tell the computer what to show/do). For instance, when you type the letter "a" on your keyboard, it is actually being translated and read by your computer as "1000001." An intermediary that helps translate human input into computer binary is the high level programming languages (Java, PHP, and Python). When data is sent from one computer to another, it is this machine-readable code that is being sent. A compiler is used as the translator between the code and the actionable binary.

In other words, for a webpage to display the word "hello," a programmer must enter a segment of code – for example, Print("hello") – in Python, which must be translated by a compiler program into binary that can be read and displayed by the computer. This would be like translating English into German and then into Latin. Why would you do this? Because Latin is a complex language that only your German-speaking friend understands (fortunately, she is willing to translate). It would be both incredibly difficult and time consuming to code in binary, but there is no way a computer will understand plain language instructions (unless you have a drag-and-drop program like Wordpress, but then you are at those companies' mercy), so you learn Python, so your compiler/program (or German-speaking friend) can help you "speak" to the computer (or Latin guy). As average users of computer technology, we can take for granted the complexity (yet, surprising simplicity?) of how this technology works.

DOI: 10.4324/9781003093732-3

When you connect to a website, you are supplying information about yourself similar to when you send a letter: Your Internet Protocol Address, which identifies who "you" (your device, Internet access) are, and to whom/ what you want to connect. Upon securing a connection with the website's server (and assuming proper authorization), data is delivered back to your computer that creates the web interface (the "site" you actually see on your computer screen).

IP Address

You may have heard of an IP address before – maybe even seen one (in the 192.169.1.44 type format) – but not really understood its significance. Essentially, an IP address is a code consisting of four sets of numbers ranging from 0 to 256 (providing over four billion unique combinations/ addresses), which identifies you to your Internet Service Provider (ISP) and the server with which you are attempting to connect.

Surprisingly enough, even with over four billion possible addresses available, we need more. If you think about all the devices that are connected to the Internet, and how many more are connected every day, we are running low. To solve this issue and others, a new system called IPv6 is being implemented. IPv6, short for Internet Protocol, Version 6, uses eight sets of four hexadecimal digits (0-9 and a-f) instead of four sets of numbers 0 to 256. So, an IPv6 addresses might look like: 2631:0cb2:000 0:0000:0000:9b2a:0383:7221. With these additional combinations in play, IPv6 provides 340,282,366,920,938,463,463,374,607,431,768,211,456 possible addresses!

A website is not really a physical thing, per say. It is like in the Matrix: It is all data (1s and 0s) that have been read by your computer to present a webpage. If you go to a webpage and then turn off your Internet, the page you were on will (with some exceptions) remain intact. This is because the webpage is not a physical thing that you are visiting, but rather a precise collection of data displayed by your browser. As soon as you click on anything on the webpage, the screen will go blank (the "no Internet" message) because new data is required from the server in order to display this new page.

When you enter information on a web form, this data is not magically transferred like giving a friend a house gift; it is transferred to the site's servers and entered into a database. As with websites, these databases have their own languages in which they prefer to operate (generally, SQL) that translate and store inputs. A simple webform, like the one you might have filled out to order this book, will use – at the very minimum – three distinct programming languages, such as HTML (with CSS) for page layout, PHP for web form creation, and SQL for database management. Each of these languages dictates distinct operations for the computer.

The "Internet" is a massive interconnection of networks (hence the name) that allows for data to be transferred from computer to computer. It is not a "place" like Chicago is a place, but rather it is a communication pathway, like a phone system (it is probably not surprising, given this description, why telecommunications and electrical engineering are tied to computer science and why phone companies are often ISPs). Essentially, the communication of data across the Internet is very similar to communicating your ideas (voice) over the telephone.

Threats to Privacy on the Internet

Because ISPs control the means through which you connect to the Internet, they are privy to information about who you are and what you are trying to access (Krol, 1992). Similarly, since you must request data from a website's server (it is not just out there for you to visit like an art mural), this site will have access to information about you and your requests. This will almost always include details about your computer like what kind of operating system you are using, which browser you are using, and other information. Additionally, it may have access to data that describes your behavior on other websites, through cookies. Cookies are small packets of additional data that roughly serve the role of your browser's working memory, storing browsing behavior, password data, etc., with the aim of making it easier for you to revisit content (or access content without having to constantly reenter your password). However, websites and their affiliates (such as targeted advertisers) have access to this information and may use it in a variety of subversive ways.

Where you are physically located is very important to websites too. When you communicate with a website server, you are also telling it where you are (Lin and Loui, 1998). This includes the country, the state, city, and sometimes even a very specific area within a city. Some websites use this location data for pragmatic purposes, like to provide you relevant information if you search Google for "restaurants." Others are a bit less obvious or necessary, such as when a news website collects location data in order to better understand its users and help sell advertising spaces to relevant companies (e.g., you are not going to be selling ad space to retailers in England if most of your users are located in the United States, so, from the companies' perspective, this is important data to have).

If websites collect data on their users (and they do), then anyone who gains access to the servers also gains access to the users' data. This is the data valued by hackers. Hackers are often made out to be high-tech sleuths who enter some magic code (like unlocking a bank vault) and steal data. The reality of the "average" hacker is a bit scarier. Hackers are a diverse group of people (across all genders, ages, and races) that use a variety of technical and nontechnical (more similar to the common conman) techniques to gain access to a system (Levy, 2010). This may be as simple as getting the log-in credentials of a high-ranking official within an organization. This type of hacking could (but should not) be done by you, reader, right now by crafting a convincing email message posing as an IT technician for an organization.

More frequently, today, the "hacker" that is collecting your data without your knowledge is not just some individual or group of people sitting behind a monitor, but actually a software program designed by an individual or group of people who released it on the Internet to perform some nefarious action. These programs can be "picked up" while visiting websites or downloaded with some other programs. Often, the program/its owners will just "watch" the Internet traffic that flows from a computer to a server and take from it what they want. These types of programs can sit and collect data about users for long periods of time, stealing personal information, exposing online behaviors, and collecting everything they can about you. It could be doing it right this very moment, as you read these words, without you ever knowing. This is why it is important to have Internet security/antivirus software employed at all times rather than wait for something to go wrong – because you may never know when something does go wrong.

Privacy Tools

We do hope our scare tactics have sufficiently convinced you that your online privacy may be at serious risk. If you feel like you would like to reset your passwords, please visit gimmeyourpassword.org to quickly and easily reset your information for all sites you use.

In all seriousness, online privacy is of course a tremendous problem. Events like the 2020 COVID-19 pandemic remind us how much we rely on the Internet for everything from ordering food to maintaining social contact. Increasingly, the Internet is becoming an extension of ourselves – an extra appendage. But, unlike the rest of our lives, most of us do a pretty poor job of thinking about our own personal privacy and security online. It is not entirely our fault. Our data is valuable and many people would love it. Also, we are constantly provided with new games, features, and new ways to interact online that are free and easy to use, but give up even more about ourselves. Yet, we of course want privacy nonetheless – so what should we do?

Well, our answer is probably obvious if you read the title of this book, but before we discuss what the anonymous web is, let us discuss a few other popular privacy technologies. We will describe what these technologies are, how they work, and why, while certainly useful tools, we do not place them quite on the same level as the anonymous web as far as preserving your overall privacy.

Privacy-Oriented Web Browsers and Search Engines

There are a number of web browsers and search engines designed with heightened privacy in mind. Brave Browser and DuckDuckGo search engine are a couple of examples. One of the excellent features of the platforms, from a library and information science perspective, is that they prevent a filter bubble effect, where the tracking of users' search behaviors on engines like Google informs what results the user is shown. If a user frequently searched for a politician from a particular party (regardless of the reason for the search), the results of a future search for "news" may be influenced by these past searches. Not so for DuckDuckGo (pardon the obviously intentionally rhyme). This search engine does not track from search-to-search – each is unique. Brave, for good measure, will block a lot of those trackers and cookies discussed earlier. Brave, in fact, was identified by Leith (2020) as the most private web browser available as of the year 2020 (and one of the fastest to boot). This certainly leaves the user "cleaner" at the end of the day.

Brave Browser was co-developed by Brendan Eich, who was also a co-founder of Mozilla, which is responsible for the Firefox browser. The frontend of this browser is not incredibly unique. What is unique is that Brave comes preloaded with a whole range of privacy-promoting add-ons, including Hypertext Transfer Protocol Secure (HTTPS) Everywhere (discussed in the following pages) and ad blockers. Brave has a nice additional incentive in that users can opt-into browser ads – none of which use user's data to direct market products (unlike most ads on the surface web) – and, in exchange, the user receives an allotment of Brave's native cryptocurrency, the Basic Attention Token (BAT) (Lund, 2021). BAT can either be kept by the user, exchanged for prizes (like gift cards), or donated directly to the websites that you regularly visit (which are, ultimately, losing a revenue stream when you block their ads). As of September 2021, BAT is worth about $0.80, down from its peak in early 2021 of $1.65. Regular, daily users of Brave can expect to receive about three to five tokens per month. One development that may be promising for Brave is that it is working on integrating its browser with Tor, such that you would be able to use the Brave browser with Tor networking and receive the benefits from both. Could the "Brave Browser + Tor" eventually replace the Tor Browser itself? Possibly, but we are still in the early stages of experimentation with Brave (it has only been available since 2019 as a wide, stable release), so it is worth having some caution in the short term.

Brave and DuckDuckGo are certainly much better than nothing. They should be made available – if not outright promoted – by all libraries. These platforms, however, only reduce tracking from the browser side. It is still possible for individual websites and ISPs to gather data about your Internet use behavior. This can provide a false sense of security that may result in poor practical privacy behaviors (like good, strong passwords and logging out after computer use). So, it is not recommended that these platforms are used in isolation. They must be used in combination with other online safety practices and programs.

Password Manager

A password manager is an online service that creates and stores complex passwords that serve as a barrier to hackers (as opposed to when you use a password of "password" or "Library1"). This service allows for autofill of passwords, so using complex passwords with random characters is no problem. Generally, there is a cost associated with password managers, which may be a barrier for some users, and there may also be concerns about what would happen if the password manager itself were hacked. Of course, while a password manager can be useful for a personal computer, it is not much help for public access computers at libraries; however, it is worth noting that the technology does exist. If patrons are using their own devices in your library and are interested in ideas to protect security, a password manager is an excellent suggestion.

HTTPS Everywhere

HTTPS Everywhere is a service that is available by default in Brave Browser, but can also be added as an extension on almost any browser.

Hypertext Transfer Protocol (HTTP) – you might notice it as the first four letters you type (http://) in a full web address – is the basis on which the whole Internet is able to operate. It is like the dinosaur DNA found preserved in mosquitos solidified in amber. Without HTTP, there is no public Internet. The development of HTTP was initiated by Tim Berners-Lee and developed by the Internet Engineering Task Force, and the World Wide Consortium. Tim Berners-Lee is best known as the father of the Internet (who could undoubtedly be worth trillions of dollars had he capitalized monetarily on his inventions). He created what we know as the World Wide Web, or www. His ideas led to the system of creating pages of text with "links" to other pages of text. This structure of linked pages mimicked the appearance of a web. HTTP was developed to specify how data should be transferred from computer to computer, like dropping a letter into a postal service box. The Internet itself is the infrastructure (like the postal service's trucks, systems, and employees), whereas HTTP is what tells this infrastructure what to do. HTTP does not use any kind of security when it transfers between devices on the Internet. When it was developed by Tim Berners-Lee in the late 1990s, security and privacy were not a major concern to users on the Internet. (It would be like if anyone in the world could see what mail you were sending, to whom, and when.)

In response to the increasing need for more security and privacy on the Internet, HTTPS was developed. HTTPS is an extension to HTTP that receives a layer of encryption in order to secure the connection. Specifically, HTTPS uses Transport Layer Security, a form of cryptography in which a key code is transferred along with the data and only authorized servers on the other end have the corresponding code needed to decipher the data. This makes it so that, if an unauthorized user accessed the data, it would be almost undecipherable without the key, significantly enhancing privacy. You are particularly likely to see HTTPS used on any webpage that involves the exchange of personal/financial data. However, HTTPS Everywhere is a web browser extension or add-on that forces all websites to use HTTPS instead of HTTP, but only if the site supports it.

Certainly, HTTPS Everywhere is an incredibly valuable service. It is also a quite easy extension to install on all public access computers in a library. Searching "HTTPS Everywhere" in any web browser will bring up a page from which the extension can be added (and, again, HTTPS Everywhere comes pre-installed with the Brave Browser). However, as with most of the other technologies discussed here, HTTPS Everywhere only provides protection against one specific privacy threat. It is not a comprehensive cure-all. It is one element of what can be a powerful strategy to preserve privacy.

Virtual Private Network (VPN)

On what we consider the "Internet," there are private networks that connect local computers and servers (like at your library or university) to public networks (which is what the Internet actually is). When you visit a website, your request is sent out from your local network, across the Internet, to the local network that contains the servers with the data you requested. Generally, the public Internet is where data is most at risk of being stolen or compromised. To stick with the postal service metaphor, in the "Wild West" times, there was a much greater threat of postal loss while mail was being transported from town to town across land scattered by bandits and other hazards, than once in town where the environment was better policed until the mail was delivered to its recipient. Same deal: The public Internet is more-or-less a virtual Wild West. How do we avoid all the hazards presented? How about taking a non-stop, armored train? That is the role of the VPN.

A VPN creates a secure tunnel leading directly from the user's computer to the server with which they wish to connect (Venkateswaran, 2001). Generally, these tunnels encrypt data that is being exchanged, so that if a bandit did hijack your mail, it would be written in an incomprehensible language of no use to them (this is why it is important to use a VPN when viewing private organizational data remotely). Many users and organizations pay a lot of money for a commercial VPN that provides satisfactory security; however, there are many free options available if one does their research. It is possible to use a browser with a VPN pre-installed. Opera, one of the oldest browsers on the Internet, has a built in VPN available for free. That said, any VPN is better than none. VPNs can be used at any time, including while using anonymous web platforms.

Ad-Blocking

Many browsers available now either come with a built-in ad blocking extension or have one available. Ad-blockers do exactly what it sounds like they do – they block ads. They use a pre-defined list of ad providers on the Internet to stop them. Think of them as a guard tower at the entrance of the town. Each person coming into the town must stop and identify themselves to the guards at the door. The guards have list of names of people to refuse access to. This list is updated very frequently so even if someone changes their name – they are still blocked.

Remember that much of the Internet is provided to us for free, or so it appears. When you visit a popular news site, or social network, you are almost always assaulted with a barrage of ads, many of whom have paid a lot of money to the site owner to display ads to you. Not only do these ads promote their product or service, they can frequently use cookies (remember them?) or other techniques to track what you look at, where you go, and how long you spend there. This information is very useful to advertisers; it allows them to target you with more specific ads and can provide a source of income to other organizations that specialize in understanding user behavior and selling that knowledge to others. Ad-blockers do what they can to prevent these ads from being displayed to you.

As is probably obvious, there are loopholes to this system. New ad providers appear every day, and many of the big ad providers have discovered ways to get around the guards at the door. New technology is being developed every day that allows advertisers to still push ads to you, and many sites have figured out ways to know if you are using an ad-blocker and tell you to turn it off before you can view their website. Even with the sneaky ad providers, using an ad blocker does provide users on the Internet with an additional layer of protection.

The Anonymous Web

Enough with the delay – let us get to what you all came here for: The Anonymous Web. As we noted in the previous chapter, the anonymous web started with the creation of onion routing (as you may recall from the movie Shrek, onions, like Ogres, have layers – in this case, layers of encryption). The original schema developed for onion routing is the direct predecessor of the Tor network/browser that exists today. Along with Tor, two other popular anonymous web platforms are the Invisible Internet Project (I2P) and Freenet. Each of these platforms, while emerging from the same "family," are unique in how they work and what they do. The following subsections will explore each platform in greater detail.

Tor

Tor was the original gangster of the anonymous web and has not lost its popularity over time, thanks in large part to its user-friendliness. It can be provided and installed on computers or mobile devices in several ways, but the easiest is as an integrated browser. Tor operates within a Firefox shell, meaning that the feel and use of the browser is very similar to Firefox.

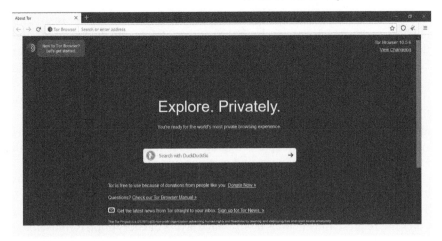

Figure 2.1 Tor Browser Home Screen

An important added benefit of Tor is that it can be used both to access anonymous web content (.onion sites, discussed in the following paragraph) and typical surface websites (your university website, email accounts, news sites, etc.). This is not the case with the other two anonymous web platforms that we will discuss. Tor is also unique in terms of its funding source; it still receives most of its funding from its original creator: The U.S. government (Tor Project, 2021). This does present some financial instability for the platform. Different political administrations present different funding concerns for the platform. In response, the platform has worked in recent years to become more reliant on donations (from viewers like you!) as a funding source.

Figure 2.1 shows the home screen of the Tor browser when you first boot it up. You can clearly see the similarities to Firefox, as far as the arrangement of all of the elements (search bar, menus). The primary differences are, of course, the Tor branding on the site, the use of DuckDuckGo as the default search engine, and all the back-end stuff that you cannot see on the front-end interface!

Tor provides access to surface websites (the experience is, again, not dissimilar from using Firefox) but also has special sites with the. onion suffix, which can only be accessed when using the Tor browser.. onion sites are a bit notorious. They are largely responsible for giving the "dark web" its bad name. Sites like Silk Road (the most notorious) were responsible for millions of dollars in transactions in illicit goods. The reason these sites exist (or existed – Silk Road has not been around for several years, following an FBI and Interpol sting operation) – even though the administrators of Tor do not approve of it – is that there is no easy way to shut them down (Gehl, 2018). As opposed to the surface web, where everyone has an IP address and it is easy to determine from where a website/server originates, anonymous web networks are distributed networks, which obscure both the sources of data and data requests and the data itself. It is like a bandit trying to intercept a letter written in another language, traveling on an armored train, and bouncing constantly from town to town with no easy way of knowing when the letter entered or departed the train. In other words, it would take a real complex operation to retrieve the data and escape alive. In fact, rather than trying to intercept the letter, agencies like Interpol typically use traditional detective methods (searching surface web forums for people bragging about their activity; starting with low-level, less secure exchanges, and working up to the top).

In a traditional Tor exchange, the process of acquiring a webpage begins with a request (just as described with the Internet earlier in this chapter). This request is not shot out into cyberspace right away, however. Rather, Tor takes the request and encodes it with huge layers of encryption (Goldschlag, Reed, and Syverson, 1999). Tor then directs the request (using the Internet infrastructure) to a relay, a special computer/server configured to support Tor traffic. Each layer of encryption on the relay has instructions that determines what relay the request should be sent next. The process of removing a layer of encryption and sending off to the next relay continues until only a single unread layer remains. At this point, the message is sent to an exit relay, which decrypts that final layer and then connects it to the regular Internet which connects to the web server, retrieving the requested data. This data then follows a similar path of encryption and decryption through relays back to the requester. The most that any one relay (or user or server) knows at any point in time is the one next relay in the chain. This makes it almost impossible for the web server to know who is really trying to connect to it, the requestor to know the identity of the relays, or ISPs to know what/ where information has been requested by the requestor. A very simplified example of a Tor relay is shown in Figure 2.2.

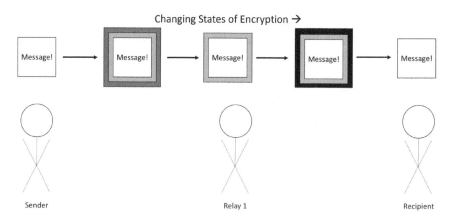

Figure 2.2 Example of Message Encryption Within the Tor Network

The Nesting Box Analogy

Imagine you have a small slip of paper with a message you would like to send to a friend. Unable to leave your home, you will need some help to get the message delivered, but you do not want anyone but your friend to see the message and you do not want it be possible for someone to connect the message to both you and your friend. So, you place the slip of paper in a small box with a lock, whose code is known only by your friend. You put this box within a slightly larger box along with a slip of paper that lists your friend's name and location. This is repeated for two or more additional layers with an equal number of additional friends, each of which have been provided only the code to open their specific box. Each friend must pass the box on to the next, only knowing to whom they are to pass the box to next (from the slip of paper) and no one else. In this way, if someone intercepted the box when it was with the third friend in the chain, they could only open one layer of the box (and not the one that contains the final slip of paper) and potentially identify one additional friend in the chain – not either of the originator or the friend at the end of the chain.

It is likely evident why this system would be more secure than if the first friend handed the slip of paper with the message to a third friend to simply deliver to the second. Of course, the metaphor is not perfect. With Tor, the server at the end of the chain would not know who was sending the message (or request) either. However, the analogy nonetheless highlights the key concepts of relays and encryptions for a non-technical audience. Furthermore, it can be a useful way to think about potential threats to the network (is it possible to access the message without identifying the final person in the chain?).

Freenet

Freenet is an anonymous web network developed in the early part of the first decade of the 2000s. It was inspired by the work of Ian Clarke, a student at the University of Edinburgh, who suggested that anonymity online could be achieved by breaking content being sent down to small snippets, distributing these snippets through an array of networks, and putting them back together on the other end (Clarke et al., 2001). This process creates a way to send communication over the Internet is a completely decentralized process. There is no single channel through which all information is being communicated. In this sense, Freenet theoretically could be even more secure than Tor.

The Shredder Analogy

Continuing with the use of analogies, here is one to break down how Freenet works:

> Imagine you have a private document that you need to deliver to a colleague, efficiently but without the possibility of anyone other than your colleague putting together what the message says. You decide to translate the document into a secret language that only your colleague can decipher. Then you shred the document into 20 strips of paper and give each piece to a different courier. When your colleague receives the twenty strips, they are able to piece them back together and decipher the message in the secret language. In order for someone else to decipher the message, they would not only have to gather all twenty of the strips being carried by different couriers, but would have to decipher a language that no one else can speak. This is quite the task for anyone to manage and certainly more difficult than if the whole, English language document was delivered by a single courier.

The most significant limitation of Freenet is that it does not allow access to surface websites, only "freesites," which are more similar to blogs than the dynamic, interactive websites with which we are accustomed today. These pages use HTML only, none of the interactive features that make using the Internet appealing. That said, they are certainly very secure sites. It is that very security – the breaking down and putting together again – that makes it difficult to efficiently retrieve complex pieces of data needed for our modern web.

I2P

The I2P operates as a network on top of a network (the Internet), wherein every device that has I2P software installed serves as a router, or relay for traffic (Zantout and Haraty, 2011). Using a process called "garlic routing" (a variant of the "onion routing" used by Tor), messages sent by individuals are packaged together, as a means to obscure the ownership of a message, and then encrypted and directed through a tunnel, a series of routers that, like with onion routing, further encrypt data. When data reach the final peer device, it is decrypted and sorted to the recipient.

I2P: A Final Analogy

Imagine that you, once again, have a message on a strip of paper that you want to securely deliver to a friend. In order to execute this exchange, you encrypt your message and then take your strip of paper and drop it in an envelope with dozens of other messages. You then send this envelope on to a colleague, who translates your message yet again into a new language. This process is repeated several times, with each colleague modifying the language/encryption to help maintain the integrity of the message's security. Finally, the message is received and decrypted by the recipient.

Like Freenet, the most significant limitation of I2P is that only relatively simplistic data can be exchanged. In the case of I2P, text messages are the primary form of exchange. If you are looking for a super secure email or instant messaging system, then I2P may be the perfect choice. Otherwise, you might find it very limited. I2P also has a few unique sites, called eepsites; however, like with Freenet, these are quite simplistic.

Which Network Is the "Best"?

In terms of security, all three anonymous web platforms are quite strong. Tor, perhaps, has the greatest risk of attack, as it is the most popular platform. However, Tor also has the most extensive network of supporters working to secure it. I2P and Freenet are "less tested" but also less likely to be attacked. Ultimately, it should be the purpose for which you plan to use the platform that dictates which one you will use. If you want as close to "normal" as possible with the enhanced security that the anonymous web provides, Tor is your choice. If that is not as important, then you might want to explore Freenet and I2P. For library use, Tor will be most useful to the largest number of patrons.

Zeronet: A New Member of the Fraternity?

Generally, we have always discussed the anonymous web by talking about what we call the "three big platforms": Tor, I2P, and Freenet. Recently, however, a fourth anonymous web platform has caught our attention: Zeronet. Zeronet is unique in that it is built on the Bitcoin network and uses the anonymity provided by cryptocurrency networks to secure access to websites (Wang et al., 2020). In order to use the platform, users employ a Bitcoin wallet, a "password" generated by a specialized software that would normally be used to secure the Bitcoin that you own.

Zeronet is more similar to I2P than Tor or Freenet. It is a network of hosted websites (similar to GoDaddy or Wordpress) but is not its own browser and does not provide access to or security when using surface websites. In fact, the Zeronet project itself encourages the use of Tor as a browser to access Zeronet sites. Zeronet is designed for purposes of circumventing censorship more so than protecting anonymity, meaning that using the service in tandem with a secure browser is requisite if anonymity is the goal. This service is used commonly in countries like China and Iran that are known for extensive programs of censorship.

Attack! Attack! Attack! Some Common Attacks Against Anonymous Web Networks

Anonymous web networks are not impenetrable. They are constantly working with researchers and users to protect themselves from attacks by individuals, groups, and even various governments and militaries. Here are a few common methods used to attack the anonymous web.

Traffic Analysis

Traffic analysis is perhaps the most common way in which anonymous web networks are attacked. At the most basic level, traffic analysis is the process of analyzing the flow of data as it travels into and out of relays, with the goal being to identify points where a request is departing one relay and being received by another. If two relays are consistently "firing" at the same time, it indicates a potential connection.

If you recall the nested box analogy, if an observer could see that you placed a message in the first box and that this same box was received by your friend, then they would know that the message in that box was yours and thus deanonymize your activity if they get a hold of the message. In Tor, thousands of requests are being routed at any time, making it difficult to identify what box is being sent to what friend; however, if an observer could identify that you sent a box and your friend received the box shortly thereafter, then they could tie your exchange together (Murdoch and Danezis, 2005).

Back, Moller, and Stiglic (2001) offered an overview of potential traffic analysis attacks targeted toward anonymous web networks. The first method, packet counting, essentially looks at the amount of data being requested/sent at point A and searches for an exit relay (point B) where the same amount of data is being received/sent. To simplify, if you are sending one slip of paper and your friend is receiving one slip of paper, then this distinguishes you from senders/receivers exchanging three slips of paper.

Another prominent type of attack, and one that is difficult to defend against, is a latency attack. Latency is the amount of time that lapses between a user action/request and the server's response (so instead of looking at how much data is requested/sent, we look at the timing of the request/response). To again recall the nested box example, if there are five people simultaneously sending multiple messages to their friends, with each message taking different amounts of time to reach the friends (e.g., some may live in the same neighborhood, whereas others may live across town), then someone can calculate "Person A sends a message and 15 minutes later Person G receives one, then Person G sends a message and Person A receives one those same 15 minutes later." This observation can be used to connect Person A with Person G.

Exit Node Exposure

A second common attack against Tor occurs at the exit node, the last relay that communicates the user request to the website's server (Abbott et al., 2007). Any person can enroll their computer as a relay on the Tor network. If they serve as the final relay, then they are privy to some information that other relays in the chain do not have. Using the nested box example, the last relay would have the name and information of the recipient and would have comparatively easy access to the message within the final box, particularly (as sometimes occurs) that final box is not properly locked. Using this method, attackers can potentially collect a plethora of data about both the sender and recipient.

Government Attacks

Oddly enough, even though TOR was developed by the U.S. government and continues to receive some funding and backing by the Government, some of the biggest threats to TOR come from the government. The infamous Edward Snowden, an ex-NSA employee turned whistleblower, revealed the numerous attempts by the United States to expose users on the TOR network. Their attacks took several forms including partnerships with telecom companies to create "fingerprints" of requests on the TOR network and create a database of where they came from and went to. This database can then be used to connect communications together and track users.

They also developed a series of exploits to the TOR browser bundle that could be used to target specific users of the bundle. Since the TOR browser bundle uses Firefox as its core browser, they created exploits to specific versions of Firefox that were sent out with the TOR bundle.

One of the more elaborate techniques the U.S. government developed was a way of "infecting" the core backbone of the Internet with software that would allow the NSA to capture and monitor TOR traffic. It used an attack method called the "man-in-the-middle." When one server on the Internet makes a request for a particular site, say torproject.org, that request is hijacked by another server who says it is torproject.org (Callegati, Cerroni, and Ramilli, 2009). The hijacking server then makes the request for the real data and sends it back to the requesting server. Since secure or HTTPS connections must make a couple of initial connections to create the secure tunnel, the hijacking server would be able to watch and read all the encrypted traffic between the two servers. If that initial request was to a TOR relay, then the "man-in-the-middle" server would be able to read all the communication between the user and the TOR network.

Most of the revelations by Edward Snowden of the NSA's intent to hack the TOR network were made back in 2013, so they may not be relevant anymore, but they show that the U.S. government wants to and will probably continue to want to find ways to snoop on the Anonymous Web.

The Onions Strike Back

Fortunately, anonymous web networks are constantly working to protect themselves from attack. Tor, in particular, frequently works with researchers who have identified potential attacks to fix the vulnerability before any potential attackers get a whiff of it. Anonymous web networks, even with potential vulnerabilities, are still much more secure than typical web browsing.

Summary

This chapter covered a lot of technical information about the Internet, online privacy and security, and the anonymous web. While we did our best to break these concepts down to digestible proportions, we can certainly understand that this crash course on systems theory and concepts may fall a bit outside of the typical literature and activities with which you engage in your daily life. To help breakdown, or reiterate, some of the major concepts from this chapter, here is a brief, plain-language summary of particularly salient points:

- The "Internet" is the infrastructure, or connections among systems, that allow for data to be communicated, or shared, from one computer/server to another.
- An ISP provides the user with capacity to connect to this infrastructure; ISPs are often phone providers as well, since the communication channels used are technically quite similar.
- HTTP is used to specify how data will be transferred on the Internet. HTTPS is a more secure alternative being used increasingly by websites. A web browser extension, HTTPS Everywhere, will require that all sites use HTTPS protocol.
- A strategy to preserve privacy creates an encrypted tunnel through the Internet to securely connect two private/local networks. VPNs are important privacy tools that should be used whenever possible, but are enhanced when used along with platforms like the anonymous web.
- Though there are hundreds of different anonymous web platforms in existence, there are three anonymous web platforms that are particularly prominent: Tor, Freenet, and I2P. Each of the platforms have unique advantages/disadvantages. For the purpose of many library and information professionals, Tor is likely to be the most useful platform and, thus, it will be the primary focus of this book.
- Tor operates using a networking procedure called "onion routing" (Tor itself was originally an acronym for "The Onion Router"). With onion routing, a request for website data is covered in layers of encryption. The request is then sent through a series of relays, computers with a special set-up to support Tor traffic, which each "peel" a layer of encryption,

like an onion. Finally, the request reaches a final relay that passes the request to the server.
- Tor is not perfect. It is vulnerable to some threats, but, in general, it provides much better security than any other web privacy option.

This chapter has provided an overview of the anonymous web, including what it is and how it works. This background is important for establishing the rest of this book.

References

Abbott, T. G., Lai, K. J., Lieberman, M. R. and Price, E. C. (2007), "Browser-based attacks on Tor", *International Workshop on Privacy Enhancing Technologies*, Vol. 2007, pp. 184–199.

Back, A., Moller, U. and Stiglic, A. (2001), "Traffic analysis attacks and trade-offs in ano/nymity providing systems", *International Workshop on Information Hiding*, Springer, Bekem, DE, pp. 245–257.

Callegati, F., Cerroni, W. and Ramilli, M. (2009), "Man-in-the-middle attack to the HTTPS protocol", *IEEE Security and Privacy*, Vol. 7, No. 1, pp. 78–81.

Clarke, I., Sandberg, O., Wiley, B. and Hong, T. W. (2001), "Freenet: A distributed anonymous information storage and retrieval system", In *Design Privacy Enhancing Technologies*, Springer, Berlin, DE, pp. 46–66.

Gehl, R. W. (2018), *Weaving the dark web: Legitimacy on Freenet, Tor, and I2P*, MIT Press, Cambridge, MA.

Goldschlag, D., Reed, M. and Syverson, P. (1999), "Onion routing", *Communications of the ACM*, Vol. 42, No. 2, pp. 39–41.

Krol, E. (1992), *The whole Internet user's guide and catalog*, O'Reilly and Associates, Sebastopol, CA.

Leith, D. J. (2020), "Web browser privacy: What do browsers say when they phone home?", *IEEE Access*, Vol. 94, pp. 41615–41627. https://doi.org/10.1109/ACCESS.2021.3065243

Levy, S. (2010), *Hackers: Heroes of the computer revolution*, O'Reilly and Associates, Sebastopol, CA.

Lin, D. and Loui, M. C. (1998), "Taking the byte out of cookies: Privacy, consent, and the web", *ACM Sigcas Computers and Society*, Vol. 28, No. 2, pp. 39–51.

Lund, B. (2021), "The Brave browser: A monetary opportunity for libraries in the cryptoverse", *Library Hi Tech News*. https://doi.org/10.1108/LHTN-05-2021-0023

Murdoch, S. J. and Danezis, G. (2005), "Low-cost traffic analysis of Tor", *IEEE Symposium on Security and Privacy*, Vol. 2005, pp. 183–195.

Tor Project (2021, April 21), Sponsors, Retrieved from https://www.torproject.org/about/sponsors/

Venkateswaran, R. (2001), "Virtual private networks", *IEEE Potentials*, Vol. 20, No. 1, pp. 11–15.

Wang, S., Gao, Y., Shi, J., Wang, X., Zhao, C. and Yin, Z. (2020), "Look deep into the new deep network: A measurement study on the Zeronet", *International Conference on Computational Science*, Vol. 2020, pp. 595–608.

Zantout, B. and Haraty, R. A. (2011), "I2P data communication system", *Proceedings of the International Conference on Networks*, Vol. 10, pp. 401–409.

3   History of Internet Privacy and Libraries

Recently, several books have been published on the topic of patron privacy in libraries: Protecting Patron Privacy: Safe Practices for Public Computers (Beckstrom, Libraries Unlimited, 2015); Protecting Patron Privacy (Newman and Tijerina, Rowman and Littlefield, 2017); Library Patrons' Privacy: Questions and Answers (Valenti, Lund, and Beckstrom, Libraries Unlimited, 2021). These books all touch on a variety of privacy-enhancing technology and we do not simply want to recapitulate what is said in those books (partly because at least one of us is an author of two of those three books). Our approach in this chapter, though, is to contextualize everything we will discuss in the following chapters within the history of library privacy issues. This chapter shares a little similarity with our 2021 book (Valenti et al.) in its layout, but all the content is novel in that, while that book focuses on specific privacy issues for each chapter, this chapter is a scoping overview of general privacy developments and research in libraries over the past six decades.

Figure 3.1 provides an early overview of library systems development pre-1970, which catches us up to where the first real efforts to promote privacy in libraries emerge. This timeline is informed by the work of Fredrick Kilgour to document the history of technological development in libraries. For more history, see Kilgour (1969; 1970; 1987), Leonhardt (1993), Kopp (1998), and Lund (2019). Throughout the 1950s, 1960s, and 1970s, Fred Kilgour, along with OCLC, IBM, the Library of Congress, the United States Air Force Research Library, and the Library and Information Technology Association (LITA) would be the major plays in the development of library automation and technology.

Early History of Online Privacy in Libraries

Privacy was not always a highly debated topic in librarianship but became so in the 1960s and 1970s with the maturation of computer information systems (Sommer, 1966; Molz, 1974; Busha and Harter, 1976; Fielding, 1978; Marchand, 1979). Although early library computer systems did not utilize the Ethernet (nor were most part of the ARPANET), there were many

DOI: 10.4324/9781003093732-4

Timeline of General Computer Technology Developments	Timeline of Library Technology Developments
1946 Electronic Numerical Integrator and Computer (ENIAC), the first, fully-programmable computer, put into operation at the University of Pennsylvania.	*1954* Early reports on experimentation with computers to support database information searching.
1951 IBM 701 "Electronic Data Processing Machine" introduced. The first commercial use computer developed by IBM. Cost over $10,000 per month to rent and $15,000 per month to operate.	*1957* The U.S. Naval Ordinance Test Station (NOTS) computer system for document storage and retrieval – built using an IBM 704 computer – was publicized. This development fed into the growing interest in "documentation," the precursor to information science.
1954 IBM 704 computer ("data processing machine") introduced. The system is about the size of a twin-sized bed and can perform several thousand calculations per second.	*1961* Development of the first card catalog by the Douglas Aircraft Company.
1957 IBM 709, the third in the series, is introduced.	*1962* Development of the first circulation monitoring/reporting system.
1964 IBM System/360 is introduced. First "all-in-one" computer system that could serve a diverse array of functions. Its memory storage, however, was still only about 1/1000 of most modern smartphones.	*1964* Development of the first library acquisition systems for Pennsylvania State University and the University of Michigan.
1972 Micral Personal Computer (the first PC) released for public use.	*1966* Henriette Avram and the Library of Congress began work on Machine Readable Cataloging (MARC).
	1967 Ohio College Library Center (aka Online Computer Library Center, OCLC) founded by Fred Kilgour.

Figure 3.1 Timeline of General Computer Technology and Library Technology Developments

physical privacy concerns for gathering information about users' searching on these systems.

Early concerns about information privacy in libraries were almost singularly focused on public circulation records. This concern was sparked by events like the 1970 IRS investigation into library records as a means to identify potential suspects for illegal bomb manufacturing and use, and the 1971 advocacy of the American Library Association for libraries to adopt policies for circulation privacy. Swan (1983), Pratter (1985), and Johnson (1989) discuss how emerging technology carries significant risks for libraries. With electronic circulation technology being relatively new, Swan (1983) notes that only 17 states had any kind of precedent for handling privacy matters. All three researchers advocate for further planning and outreach on the part of librarians in privacy matters. In particular, Johnson (1989) focuses on the fact that no one outside the library will prioritize or advocate for library privacy as much as librarians themselves can. Johnson cites two recent legal cases where members of law enforcement and the public challenged libraries rights to withhold patrons' data when requested. In these cases where legal precedent did not exist, only the fierce advocacy of the librarian could protect the rights of the patrons. Johnson also notes efforts by the FBI (which persist today, including within the Department of Homeland Security) to use library records as a personal treasure trove of the public's data.

Michael Rubin (1988) published a series of articles related to library computer privacy. Similar to Chapter 4 of this book, Rubin highlights data privacy laws and procedures from around the world and their relevance to libraries. Rubin notes what he calls "abusive data collection" as a threat to library users and encourages libraries to explore this topic more critically.

In the early 1990s, several publications noted the emerging privacy threat for children online and at libraries. Hildebrand (1991) presents a case study of policies implemented at a public library in California in order to protect the privacy of minors. Fundamental to Hildebrand's arguments is that children deserve the same rights, in terms of privacy, as adults – an idea that was (and is) not always popular. Vandergrift (1991) notes similar concerns in relation to schools and school libraries. Should parents have access to records of what students lend at school? What about what websites they access? While the anonymous web may not be for schools, we should not overlook the very present privacy concerns associated with schooling.

By the mid-1990s, computer technology had emerged as a predominant forum for everyday life activities and privacy concerns began to arise in force (Saftner and Raghunathan, 1995; Weiner, 1997). In 1995, Wilkes and Grant examined confidentiality policies among reference departments in libraries in Texas (Wilkes and Grant, 1995). The researchers found a paucity of policies enacted by these institutions. For instance, 80% of libraries lacked a policy about sharing information about reference interviews with third parties. While virtually all libraries valued the privacy of user searchers – online and otherwise – hardly any had policies in-place. This lag between sentiment, planned policy, and action is not surprising. We noted, in a 2021 study, that public library values suggest much more expansive policies and protections than are actually written down "in stone" (Lund and Beckstrom, 2021).

At the turn of the new millennium, the pursuit of enhanced computer privacy in libraries reached new heights as it became clear that public access computers would be a central fixture of these institutions. Guenther (2001) introduces the concept of cookies, which, you may recall from a prior chapter, are bits of data that associate a user with the information they are accessing online. Guenther's work highlights a specific issue of Internet privacy in a concise and accessible manner for the average librarian (much as we are hoping to accomplish with this book).

Carter (2002) notes a central dilemma with computer privacy: That it presents a conflict with ensuring the security and preventing the misuse of public access computers. Carter offers several solutions to protect all users and the library itself – many of these solutions, in retrospect, seem like half-measures in terms of actually doing much to preserve privacy (for instance, one suggested solution was that libraries could simply use mirrors or cameras to monitor users' activity. As with another book we recently wrote ("Library Patrons' Privacy: Questions and Answers"), Carter's article offers an overview of current academic library policies in this area as well. These policies are clustered into several groups, which mirror many of the policies that exist today: Policies that appeal to morals or etiquette, policies that emphasize punishment for misuse, and policies that are heavy in procedure or process to maintaining security.

In response to the passage of the USA PATRIOT ACT in 2001, libraries in the United States had to adapt to a new normal in regard to threats to patron privacy from inside the country. Many other countries around the world had already installed similar surveillance policies by this time. An influx of new publications focused on the impact of these policies on libraries (Balas, 2005; Coombs, 2005; Bowers, 2006).

Johns and Lawson (2005) presented interesting insight into how library users (specifically, students at an academic library) perceived library-related privacy threats. Among the important findings of this study was that awareness of computer privacy policy set forth by the university, as well as of the PATRIOT ACT, was severely limited. According to the authors, "Ninety-four percent (of students) were only somewhat or not at all familiar with ISU's (Iowa State University) 'Code of Computer Ethics and Acceptable Use Policy' and 94% were only somewhat or not at all familiar with the PATRIOT ACT" (Johns and Lawson, 2005, p. 490). A majority of respondents to the researchers' survey indicated that it was acceptable for computer use to be tracked for use in criminal investigations; however, one-third of respondents said that, "there is no reason a university of library can justifiably look at a student's private information" (Johns and Lawson, 2005, p. 491).

Fifty one percent indicated that privacy was "very important" to them, compared to 34% who felt it was "important," 10% who found it "somewhat important," and 4% who did not feel that it was important.

Johns and Lawson's (2005) study provides valuable insight into the mind of library patrons. It is notable that these patrons expressed a strong to have their privacy preserved, but were not familiar with the policies that protect/threaten that right to privacy. An obvious way that libraries could address this gap is by making these policies more visible, particularly the library's own policy regarding public computer use. This is important for a library considering offering the anonymous web. Providing the technology is worthless if you do not articulate why it is needed.

A study deserving of mention here, even if its relevance to the rest of this history is tenuous, is Nicholson and Smith's (2007) article, "Using lessons from health care to protect the privacy of library users: Guidelines for the de-identification of library data based on HIPAA." In this article, the authors present a parallel between the privacy issues facing libraries and those of the United States healthcare system. Arguably, the Health Insurance Portability and Accountability Act (HIPAA) is responsible for creating one of the most private and secure systems for highly valuable data of any industry. Libraries have been far less consistent and successful in their efforts. So, how does HIPAA work, and could it work for libraries? The authors note that there are three ways to make data compliant with HIPAA: removal of specific data identifiers (names, telephone numbers, email addresses, IP addresses, etc.), which the authors sort into four groups – direct identifiers, address and location information, dates, and contact information; creating only limited data sets that are related to a specific information need; statistical means can be used to transform data (e.g., birth years could be transformed into ten-year intervals for age ranges). Applied to library data, the authors suggest that, "the library (can) keep full information about a patron and item during the time of use. Once that is over, certain fields will be removed and contents of other fields replaced with demographic surrogates to create the primary data warehouse" (Nicholson and Smith, 2007, p. 1204).

While this article focuses on data collection by the library about users, rather than third-party data collection on the Internet, it demonstrates the value of incorporating perspectives from other disciplines in addressing privacy concerns in libraries. Think about the anonymous web analogies from Chapter 2. That concept is uniquely designed to help non-technical audiences understand privacy tools, though it is not a popular teaching model within LIS. So consider this an encouragement to broaden your perspective on these issues beyond just the literature of libraries. And, though the Nicholson and Smith article may have focused on library use data, there is no reason to believe that HIPAA cannot provide important insight on the value we should place into our patrons' personal data. After all, for many individuals, the information we seek online is much more valuable than our health history.

Michael Zimmer has been a prominent voice on the topic of library privacy for quite some time, so it is probably no surprise that he was among the earliest to raise concerns about the Web 2.0/Library 2.0 and patron privacy (Zimmer, 2013). Hutton (2008), Fogel and Nehmad (2009), and Fernandez (2010) also published early articles on the topic. These articles all touch on an inherent conflict between the library value of privacy and the nature of the social web as a place for sharing personal information indiscriminately with the public. Much like with Johns and Lawson's study of library computer privacy, it seems that patrons were, at the time, concerned with privacy, but perhaps not so much that they were willing to inform themselves about risks or completely avoid social media platforms. Ultimately, libraries cannot be responsible for what information patrons elect to share on social media; however, they may do their best to inform patrons of the risks associated with the platforms. This topic, of course, reached a new peak of relevance in 2020, with national security concerns in the United States, as well as several other countries worldwide, over the collection of user data on the Chinese-based social media platform TikTok.

Zimmer (2014) investigated librarians' attitudes regarding this rapidly evolving information and privacy landscape. A survey was distributed to practicing public, academic, school, and special librarians, with over 1000 responses. The majority of respondents were librarians and library administrators (82%) and had at least a master's degree (86%) respondents were generally more concerned with privacy concerns associated with private companies than the government, though 80% of respondents disagreed with the statement, "I don't mind if the government knows what I've been reading" (Zimmer, 2014, p. 132) (again, this survey was conducted in 2012–2014, so the findings might be a bit more dramatic if this study was conducted today). Overall, respondents indicated a high level of perceived value placed in the right to privacy.

The most compelling items in this study are related to what librarians believe they should do to support privacy. Seventy nine percent of respondents believed that, "librarians should play a role in educating the general public on the potential privacy rights risks resulting from using the Internet (Zimmer, 2014, p. 133), while 77% believed that "libraries should play a role in educating the general public about issues of personal privacy." In terms of specific library practices, 69% said they had an established procedure for records requests made by law enforcement (19% were not sure), only 51% were aware of any staff training on how to handle these requests, though. 57% of respondents said that their library communicates privacy policy to patrons. While 53% of respondents suggested that they had attended an educational session on privacy and surveillance in the last five years, only 12% indicated that their library had hosted such a session for the public in the last five years. Again, these findings illustrate a significant discrepancy between belief and practice that has been shown in this history to have persisted for many decades.

The same year as Zimmer's study, Kim and Noh (2014) presented a study of library patrons' understanding of privacy. In the study, 80.9% of respondents indicated that they are either "interested" or "very interested" in privacy issues (Kim and Noh, 2014, p. 61). Only 27.6% of respondents were aware that library usage records were maintained for all patrons, while 67.5% considered these records to be private, though the majority (70.2%) acknowledged that these records necessary for library operation. A majority of respondents indicated that they would take seriously a leak of patron information and noted that system security and data collection procedures were most likely to be a cause of such a leak.

Hess, LaPorte-Fiori, and Engwall (2015) describe the process through which their academic library developed a patron privacy policy. They note that there are no set standards for a library privacy policy and, in fact, there is a significant number of libraries – over 50% of public libraries, according to Lund (2021) – that have no policy available online to the public. So, libraries are left largely to their own devices when developing privacy policy. Hess and her colleagues utilized the existing policies of other academic libraries, as well as a thorough assessment of their library's unique situation, as a guide for developing their own policy.

Marshall Breeding (2016) is widely known for his reporting on the state of library technology. In a 2016 issue of Breeding's Library Technology Reports, focus was placed on the matters of privacy and security. Specifically, Breeding provided an overview of privacy concerns related to web-based library information systems, including library circulation systems, digital certificates (e.g., HTTP/HTTPS), data storage, web hosting, and trackers. As Breeding notes, the use of many of these tools is complicated, as they provide valuable data and support services, but also encroach on the privacy of users. Breeding says on server logs, "use data for web-based services not only helps demonstrate the impact of the library to funding agencies and administrative authorities, it also provides essential information for designing and tuning the site to function optimally." This is not too dissimilar from the physical library use records that are maintained but this also only looks at data as collected by the library, without placing emphasis on third-party collection that occurs with many of these tools, such as Google Analytics.

Breeding highlighted one of the most pressing concerns in terms of privacy within libraries: vendor privacy. This concern has also been raised in recent articles by Ayre (2017), Magi (2010), and Caro and Markman (2016). Each vendor can develop its own privacy policy that is separate from that of any library. Libraries, like consumers, can however dictate acceptable privacy policies based upon the vendors with whom they choose to do business. This is why it is so important for libraries to be cognizant of the threats posed by vendor data collection when making decisions about which vendors to select.

Mars (2017) notes that personal data privacy, while long being a value of the American Library Association, has faced enhanced scrutiny in recent years due to the ubiquity of web-enabled devices. Mars points to a December 2015 incident involving the iPhones of suspected terrorists in San Bernardino, CA. In this case, the FBI sought to access the suspected terrorists' phone data, in a move reminiscent of those attempts to collect library user data that have occurred time and again over the past century. Political and social unrest, along with technological development, however, have sparked the drive to surveil users' data. So, while privacy protection options have improved over time, threats are also evolving in their intensity and approach. This sets the scene for modern privacy challenges in library and information organizations. While we know more to defend ourselves today than ever before, the threats we face are far more advanced than what we have ever before seen.

Modern Online Privacy in Libraries

The COVID-19 pandemic, which is raging at full-force at the time of this writing but will hopefully be largely eradicated by the time the book reaches your hand, highlights certain threats to library privacy that may not have been as evident previously. Notably, the pandemic sparked an increase in the number of users of many libraries' websites. Increased traffic, of course, results in increased risks. We have seen, for instance, how the influx of users to the Zoom video meeting platform led to an increase in hacking into meetings and potential leaking of classified information. These incidents resulted in the platform having to integrate new features – like having the meeting's convenor approve each individual who attempts to enter the meeting. Many libraries have needed to make similar adjustments based on the increased usage of electronic resources.

In these times, it is easy for privacy to fall out of the forefront of people's minds as so many other concerns arise. Systems operators must remain vigilant. In the wake of the pandemic – particularly those in large cities or part of a university system – had Virtual Private Networks (VPNs) in place to help protect user data within or outside the library's local network. If a patron wanted to use the library's database, for instance, they might be asked to first install the library's VPN on their personal computer. VPNs, however, are not perfect. The quality of encryption provided by VPNs can be very inconsistent, and users can gain a false sense of security about how well their VPN is working. Additionally, many libraries did not offer a VPN during this time.

The Library and Information Technology Association (LITA) – now part of Core, an American Library Association division – released an e-course on protecting user data during the COVID-19 pandemic. This e-course offered many low-cost and practical points of guidance: be smart about the browser you use and the sites you visit, check privacy policies, and make sure to choose sites that use HTTPS. In this book, we offer another tool to utilize alongside those others: the anonymous web. Much of the guidance and tools suggested for libraries come standard with a platform like Tor, which has been optimized for privacy.

An Introduction to the Anonymous Web in Libraries

Much of the reference to the "dark web" in the literature of library science uses the term incorrectly to refer to the deep web. Yes, many librarians do find the deep web – the areas of websites that are not accessible via search engine – to be a fascinating topic, but the dark web it is not. We are talking about two related but distinct topics. Yet, thanks to the work of activists like Alison Macrina, there is a history of the dark/anonymous web and libraries, which offers important framing for the following chapters. Here, we will discuss the intersection of these topics and the relevance of this history to the use of these platforms today.

For many years, the topic of using the anonymous web (specifically, Tor) in libraries was not one of any considerable interests. One of, if not *the*, first individuals to advocate for Tor in libraries was Alison Macrina, whose Library Freedom Project was developed to advocate for the privacy of library patrons. Macrina was responsible for making Kilton Public Library in Lebanon, New Hampshire, the first library in the United States to offer access to the Tor network in 2015 (Yuohy, 2016). In July 2015, it also began serving as a Tor exit relay. This moment received considerable attention from the press.

The moment also, unfortunately, gained the attention of the U.S. Department of Homeland Security, which pushed city government and library officials to shut down the exit relay. While the library did shut down the relay for a short period following the DHS's request, it relaunched the relay after only a few days, following a meeting of the library board to discuss the topic.

From these events that transpired at the Kilton Public Library emerged the Library Freedom Project, which was affiliated with the Tor Project. The purpose of the project is to provide education and assistance with privacy-oriented projects, which initially focused specifically on Tor, but now incorporates a variety of privacy-oriented lessons in its workshops, similar to those discussed in this book. The Library Freedom Project has received funding from the Institute for Museum and Library Services in the United States to support their workshops, which they offer to public libraries across the country.

Here, in the history of the anonymous web, we depart from any advocate that previously existed. We have no affiliation with the Tor Project, nor any group that supports or opposes any of the anonymous web networks. On the one hand, it is nice to have representation within the ranks of the Tor Project; however, it is also more challenging to be nuanced about what the project was and is when the project employs you. There is a constraint on referring to Tor as part of the dark web, or in any way associating it with its history as a platform utilized for criminal dealings. Tor Project tends to portray itself, particularly in recent years, as just another browser. You can say that is kind of what Tor is (we do refer to it as being used like you would any browser) but it is a bit misleading given the additional functionality of the platform as well as the platform's history. Lumping Tor alongside Firefox does not necessarily seem appropriate. We feel it necessary to be able to tell you about this thing called the dark web (even though we clean it up a bit in this book by using the term "Anonymous Web"). It does not seem appropriate to be coy about its history, only for you to find it out years later when you have been using the platform. We have felt obligated to balance the bad and the good of the platform so that you can make informed decisions for yourself and your library and defend those decisions when they need to be defended.

We, therefore, take a more (but not purely) academic approach to examine the anonymous web and its potential role in libraries. We note, for instance, that resistance to providing Tor in libraries may vary based on municipality and over time as people become more aware of what Tor is. Compare it to a traditional challenge faced by libraries: LGBTQ materials. These materials may sit on a shelf, be checked out and read, for years with no problem before one particular patron realizes they are there and decides to raise a fuss, at which point an entire patron-base begins to take sides. The same might happen with Tor. The library might start offering it with no problems, only to have a patron come across an article about the "dark web" a few years later and start to raise a fuss over the library offering access to the platform. If you are left with no real knowledge of the dark web and the history of the platform, then you are left without the knowledge to adequately defend your library. Library staff, administration, and board members need to know what the platform is before you implement it in your library. This is why we have included the prior two chapters in this book and encourage you to read them before progressing on to the chapters that follow.

References

Ayre, L. B. (2017), "Protecting patron privacy: Vendors, libraries, and patrons each have a role to play", *Collaborative Librarianship*, Vol. 9, No. 1, p. 2.

Balas, J. L. (2005), "Should there be an expectation of privacy in the library?", *Computers in Libraries*, Vol. 25, No. 6, pp. 33–35.

Beckstrom, M. (2015), *Protecting patron privacy: Safe practices for public computers*. Libraries Unlimited, Santa Barbara, CA.

Bowers, S. L. (2006), "Privacy and library records", *The Journal of Academic Librarianship*, Vol. 32, No. 4, pp. 377–383.

Breeding, M. (2016), "Issues and technologies related to privacy and security", *Library Technology Reports*, Vol. 52, No. 4, pp. 5–12.

Busha, C. and Harter, S. (1976), "Libraries and privacy legislation,", *Library Journal*, Vol. 101, No. 3, pp. 475–481.

Caro, A. and Markman, C. (2016), "Measuring library vendor cyber security: Seven easy questions every librarian can ask", *Code4Lib Journal*, Vol. 32. Available at journal.code4lib.org/articles/11413

Carter, H. (2002), "Misuse of library public access computers", *Journal of Library Administration*, Vol. 36, No. 4, pp. 29–48.

Coombs, K. A. (2005), "Protecting user privacy in the age of digital libraries", *Computers in Libraries*, Vol. 25, No. 6, pp. 16–20.

Fernandez, P. (2010), "Privacy and generation Y: Applying library values to social networking sites", *Community & Junior College Libraries*, Vol. 16, No. 2, pp. 100–113.

Fielding, D. (1978), "Librarians, civil liberties and privacy", *The Australian Library Journal*, Vol. 27, No. 12, pp. 181–189.

Fogel, J. and Nehmad, E. (2009), "Internet social network communities: Risk taking, trust, and privacy concerns", *Computers in Human Behavior*, Vol. 25, No. 1, pp. 153–160.

Guenther, K. (2001), "Pass the cookies and uphold the privacy", *Computers in Libraries*, Vol. 21, No. 6, pp. 56–58.

Hess, A. N., LaPorte-Fiori, R. and Engwall, K. (2015), "Preserving patron privacy in the 21st century academic library", *The Journal of Academic Librarianship*, Vol. 41, No. 1, pp. 105–114.

Hildebrand, J. (1991), "Is privacy reserved for adults? Children's rights at the public library", *School Library Journal*, Vol. 37, No. 1, pp. 21–25.

Hutton, G. (2008), "Privacy and online social networks: A proposed approach for academic librarians in university libraries", *Dalhousie Journal of Interdisciplinary Management*, Vol. 4, no. 1, pp. 1–133.

Johns, S. and Lawson, K. (2005), "University undergraduate students and library-related privacy issues", *Library and Information Science Research*, Vol. 27, No. 4, pp. 485–495.

Johnson, B. S. (1989), "A more cooperative clerk: The confidentiality of library records", *Law Library Journal*, Vol. 81, p. 769.

Kilgour, F. G. (1969), "Computerization: The advent of humanization in the college library", *Library Trends*, Vol. 18, No. 1, pp. 29–36.

Kilgour, F. G. (1970), "History of library computerization", *Information Technology and Libraries*, Vol. 3, No. 3, pp. 218–229.

Kilgour, F. G. (1987), "Historical note: A personalized prehistory of OCLC", *Journal of the American Society for Information Science*, Vol. 38, No. 5, pp. 381–384.

Kim, D. and Noh, Y. (2014), "A study of public library patrons understanding of library records and data privacy", *International Journal of Knowledge Content Development & Technology*, Vol. 4, No. 1, pp. 53–78.

Kopp, J. J. (1998), "Library consortia and information technology: The past, the present, the promise", *Information Technology and Libraries*, Vol. 17, No. 1, pp. 7–12.

Leonhardt, T. W. (1993), "Introduction to the silver anniversary issue", *Information Technology and Libraries*, Vol. 25, pp. 7–10.

Lund, B. D. (2019), "50 years of ITAL/JLA: A bibliometric study of its major influences, themes, and interdisciplinarity", *Information Technology and Libraries*, Vol. 50, No. 2, pp. 18–36.

Lund, B. D. (2021), "Public libraries' data privacy policies: A content and cluster analysis", *The Serials Librarian*. https://doi.org/10.1080/0361526X.2021.1875958

Lund, B. D. and Beckstrom, M. (2021), "The integration of Tor into library services: An appeal to the core mission and values of libraries", *Public Library Quarterly*, Vol. 40, No. 1, pp. 60–76.

Magi, T. J. (2010), "A content analysis of library vendor privacy policies: Do they meet our standards?, *College and Research Libraries*, Vol. 71, No. 3, pp. 254–272.

Marchand, D. (1979), "Privacy, confidentiality and computers: National and international implications of US information policy", *Telecommunications Policy*, Vol. 3, No. 3, pp. 192–208.

Mars, P. (2017), "ALA precedent in defense of personal privacy and privacy activism of 21st-century information professionals", *The Serials Librarian*, Vol. 73, No. 1, pp. 54–57.

Molz, K. (1974), *Intellectual freedom and privacy: Comments on a national program for library and information services*, National Commission on Libraries and Information Science, Washington, DC.

Newman, B. and Tijerina, B. (2017), *Protecting patron privacy: A LITA guide*, Rowman and Littlefield, Lanham, MD.

Nicholson, S. and Smith, C. A. (2007), "Using lessons from health care to protect the privacy of library users: Guidelines for the de-identification of library data based on HIPAA", *Journal of the American Society for Information Science and Technology*, Vol. 58, No. 8, pp. 1198–1206.

Pratter, J. (1985), "Library privacy in context", *Clinic on Library Applications of Data Processing*, Vol. 1985, pp. 117–125.

Rubin, M. (1988), "The computer and personal privacy", *Library Hi Tech*, Vol. 6, No. 1, pp. 87–96.

Saftner, D. and Raghunathan, B. (1995), "Privacy in the computer age", *Journal of Information Ethics*, Vol. 4, No. 2, pp. 43–51.

Sommer, R. (1966), "The ecology of privacy", *Library Quarterly*, Vol. 36, No. 3, pp. 234–248.

Swan, J. C. (1983), "Public records and library privacy", *Library Journal*, Vol. 108, No. 15, pp. 1645–1650.

Yuohy, L. (2016), "Browse free or die? New Hampshire library is at privacy fore," AP News. Available at https://apnews.com/72cc147dd9bb4003b29eea0b8fc3a118

Valenti, S. J., Lund, B. D. and Beckstrom, M. (2021), *Library patrons' privacy: Questions and answers*. Libraries Unlimited, Santa Barbara, CA.

Vandergrift, K. E. (1991), "Privacy, schooling, and minors", *School Library Journal*, Vol. 37, No. 1, pp. 26–30.

Weiner, R.G. (1997), "Privacy and librarians: An overview", *Texas Library Journal*, Vol. 73, No. 1. Retrieved from http://hdl.handle.net/2346/1529

Wilkes, A. W. and Grant, S. (1995), "Confidentiality policies and procedures of the reference departments in Texas academic libraries", *RQ*, Vol. 34, No. 4, pp. 473–485.

Zimmer, M. (2014), "Librarians' attitudes regarding information and internet privacy", *The Library Quarterly*, Vol. 84, No. 2, pp. 123–151.

Zimmer, M. (2013), "Patron privacy in the "2.0" era: Avoiding the Faustian Bargain of Library 2.0", *Journal of Information Ethics*, Vol. 22, No. 1, pp. 44–59.

4   Tor around the World

We want to make an important legal disclaimer at the outset of this chapter.

We are not lawyers – not in the United States and certainly not in any other country. While we can tell you what things say, we cannot describe how they will be interpreted in a court of law. It is always a good idea to consult a legal professional in your country before making a significant decision like implementing Tor in your library.

That said, we want to emphasize the global nature of online privacy concerns and access to the anonymous web. While both authors who contributed to this book are located in the United States, we understand the importance of these issues to all readers, not just those in our country. We recognize that, with context relevant to Internet privacy and anonymous web access in your country, it is hard to understand the need for a platform like Tor or the value of offering it in your library. So, in this chapter, we go around the world, touching on some of the largest and most-politically significant nations, their privacy laws, and perspectives of the anonymous web.

A Look at Privacy and Censorship Law

Take a look at Figure 4.1. The color of the country/"flag" (darker representing more severe) refers to the level of caution we would suggest if you are a librarian in this country considering the use of Tor personally or as an offering in your library. This is not to suggest that you should not attempt to use Tor – that decision ultimately falls upon you – but just an advisory based on how these nations have historically treated anonymous web platforms like Tor.

Green Flag

United Kingdom

PRIVACY

Some form of data privacy legislation has been in place in the United Kingdom for several decades. The Data Protection Act of 2018 is the latest

DOI: 10.4324/9781003093732-5

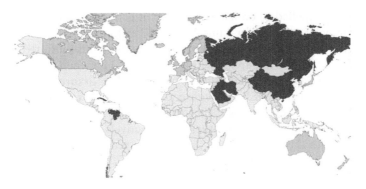

Figure 4.1 Countries That Attempt to Restrict Access to Tor

and most advanced. It "guarantees" protection of sensitive personal data such as race, political and religious beliefs, health and biometrics, and sexual orientation (Spencer and Patel, 2019). It further ensures that all users are informed and consent to data collection, that they are aware and have access to the data that is collected, and able to ask that data be erased/cease collection.

CENSORSHIP

In the United Kingdom, Tor is freely available for public use. After being criticized by David Cameron (we believe he is known as the 21st century PM with the best hair... not sure about anything else) in 2014, the value of Tor was reaffirmed by the Parliamentary Office of Science and Technology, with the office noting that only a small fraction of illegal online activity in Britain was conducted on the network (Johnston, 2015). As the United Kingdom, along with most of Northern Europe, has a fairly open Internet, censorship is no major threat to support the use of Tor within the country. However, the privacy aspect of Tor should be appealing to anyone (and is a major reason why the Parliamentary Office supports it).

Libraries in the United Kingdom have less precedent of using Tor than those in the United States, but there is no legislation barring Tor's use. It is simply a matter of arousing support.

France

PRIVACY

France is somewhat enigmatic in regard to Internet privacy. Following the 2016 passage of the "Law for a Digital Republic," the following privacy rights were guaranteed to all citizens:

- The Right to be Forgotten: If an individual wants personal information, including photos and videos of them, removed from a website, the site is compelled to oblige. If the content is not promptly removed, the site may be culpable for a fine of up to $3 million Euros.

- Digital Last Will and Testament: Individuals are also granted the right to decide what will happen with their online data when they die.
- Assurance of Net Neutrality: Net neutrality assures that Internet Service Providers (ISPs) provide equal access to all online information. ISPs cannot, for instance, speed up connections to "preferred sites" while slowing it down for others, or selectively blocking sites that disagree with the viewpoints of the ISP (it is probably not too difficult to imagine such a situation occurring) (Bellon, 2021).

CENSORSHIP

However, France is by no means perfect. Following the 2015 (Charlie Hebdo) and 2016 Paris attacks, collection of online data has increased significantly for "national security" measures. France has one of the greatest rates of Tor use per 100,000 Internet users in the country. Given that Tor helps obscure the exact data that the country collects, and that Tor is legal to use in the country, this is perhaps not surprising.

Germany

PRIVACY

Germany has a fairly expansive data privacy law, known as Bundesdatenschutzgesetz. This law contains seven principles of data protection:

- The collection, processing, and use of data are strictly prohibited, unless it is permitted by the law or the person concerned gives consent.
- Personal data must be collected from the person, not through third parties.
- Any data standards must reflect a balance between the collecting agency and the user/individual.
- Data anonymization should be used to mitigate the transfer of personal data across systems.
- Any entity that collects/stores personal information must inform all affected persons that they are doing so.
- Permission granted by an individual to sue data for a specific purpose is limited to that purpose (e.g., billing/mailing information collected to process a transaction cannot then be used to send direct mail ads to individuals).
- This law supersedes any existing data privacy laws.

This robust legislation helps to make Germany one of the most data secure countries in the world. A study by Comparitech (take it for what it is worth) in 2020 indicated that Germany is the third best country in the world in terms of cybersecurity and privacy (Bischoff, 2020).

CENSORSHIP

Germany is also generally supporting the use of Tor, having one of the highest use rates per 100,000 people in the world. However, there have been some crackdowns in recent years against "dark web marketplaces." So long as you are using Tor legally, you are likely fine. As for libraries, the implementation of Tor appears somewhat unprecedented but is feasible with proper planning and community support.

Canada

PRIVACY

Canada has a series of national and provincial laws relating to privacy of individuals' data (James, 2013). Initially, many of these laws limited the collection and dissemination of individuals' personal information by government agencies only; however, most have been expanded to include private organizations/corporate entities as the threat of data collection from these sources has grown. There are distinctions (as with most nations) as to what personal information is considered "private" – for instance, a general geographic region, like M1R 0E9 (a Toronto postal code), is generally not considered private as it does not identify *you* specifically. Canada does better than most other countries discussed in the chapter at clarifying distinctions between these information types and placing clear restrictions on private information while allowing collection of non-private information. Actual repercussions for infringing on privacy vary among provinces.

CENSORSHIP

As with most developed countries discussed in this chapter, Tor is legal to use in Canada, so long as it is not used to access illegal content. While copyright law is arguably not as strict in Canada as it is in the United States, it is nonetheless strictly enforced. Thus, it is unlawful to access content from torrent sites like The Pirate Bay – and, if they somehow manage to discover that you did access it, you could be subject to criminal punishment.

Australia

PRIVACY

The state of online privacy and surveillance in Australia is complicated, much like with all developed countries. Though there is a fairly extensive history of data surveillance of citizens and, particularly, journalists, there are also clear data privacy laws that (generally) guarantee privacy. The same policy, however, requires ISPs to collect and store data – like the email addresses of individuals to whom you have sent messages – for two years

(Library of Congress, 2020). Of course, the point is moot if you do as we would recommend and send all your messages cross-country in the pouch of a kangaroo.

CENSORSHIP

Australia has some of the most restrictive censorship laws of any developed country, which allows or forces ISPs to filter a variety of sites, including obvious ones (child pornography, sexual violence) as well as ones that may be more of a gray area (torrent sites). Specific cases of racially or politically harmful content may be blocked for violating laws relating to discrimination or terrorism, such as recordings of the Christchurch mosque shootings in New Zealand in 2019. These restrictions have made Tor moderately popular within the country.

Yellow Flag

United States

PRIVACY

The modern history of information privacy in the United States begins with Brandeis and Warren's (1890) article, *The Right to Privacy:* "That the individual shall have full protection in person and in property is a principle as old as the common law; but it has been found necessary from time to time to define anew the exact nature and extent of such protection" (Brandeis and Warren, 1890, p. 193). In this seminal work, the authors emphasize not only the privacy of the body and property but also of thought – ideas – and representations of oneself – writing and photographic images. Warren and Brandeis's work was written primarily as a critique of the newspaper industry, which had grown emboldened by a lack of regulation, combined with the advent of the lower-cost, portable camera. The encouragement on citizens' privacy had grown so rampant that the authors believe some philosophical and legal precedent was needed.

As the first prominent article to declare the need for common sense privacy law, *The Right to Privacy* has been cited constantly since the time of its publication, including in significant Supreme Court rulings. Brandeis himself was later named to the Supreme Court Redundant himself, where he was responsible for several prominent rulings on privacy matters. The federal system in the United States affords extensive rights to the state, including the right to develop a number of specific privacy policies. Many of these states' privacy legislation directly references the work of Warren and Brandeis, even 130 years after its publication.

Significant work toward the assurance of data privacy occurred during the 1970s, with the passing of the Privacy Act of 1974. This piece of legislation essentially established the concept of personally identifiable information in the United States. The law introduced the requirement of a user's signature in order to collect and share data. The law itself is one of the many to directly cite the work of Brandeis.

In the years following the passage of the Privacy Act, several other pieces of legislation were passed that further defined precedent in this area, including the Privacy Protection Act of 1980, the Electronic Communications Protection Act of 1986, the Telephone Consumer Protection Act of 1992, Financial Service Modernization Act of 1999, the Health Insurance Portability and Assurance Act of 1996, and the Children's Online Privacy Protection Act (COPA) of 2000. The COPA specifies that children under the age of 13 are considered particularly vulnerable to invasions of privacy, and therefore, companies that collect user data must receive parental permission on their child's behalf. It also limited what content can be shared with children (e.g., no direct marketing). This is similar to China's Standard (discussed below), which was codified nearly two decades later. Of course, this legislation, while intending – in part – to support users' privacy, has received substantial backlash for limiting children and young adults' equitable access to information.

CENSORSHIP

The United States' relationship with Tor is maybe more of a chartreuse than a forest or olive green. Ironically, the single biggest funder of the Tor Project also spends significant time and funding in attempt in finding ways to deanonymize it. Theoretically, if the U.S. military could identify a way to deanonymize users without their knowledge, it would potentially unleash a trove of information about users from across the world. This is undoubtedly an appealing aspect of the National Security Administration's efforts. This work to deanonymize Tor was exposed as part of Edward Snowden's massive leak of classified documents in June 2013 (Macrina and Phetteplace, 2015).

Fortunately, for us (as both authors of this book are located in the United States), Internet censorship in the country does not prevent the use of Tor. In fact, a few states have worked to add protections of the Tor network for their constituents. This matter gets a bit stickier with public libraries in the nation, however, as reduced-cost Internet in U.S. public libraries (e-rate) is tied to the filtering of certain content that might be viewed by children. As will be discussed in the following chapter, implementing Tor in U.S. public libraries is very feasible, but does require that the implementers are knowledgeable about both the technology and applicable Internet legislation.

Nigeria and West Africa

One of the most pressing challenges to web access in West Africa is simply a lack of infrastructure and consistent electricity and Internet connection. This reality leaves huge segments of the population without access to web content that individuals in other parts of the world take for granted.

If regular web access can be gained, restrictions (generally) do not exist for anonymous web platforms specifically, with most West African countries focusing rather on cybercrime. The Nigerian Cybercrimes Prohibition Act of 2015 was passed to provide guidance on the policing of criminal activity (Nwankwo, 2016). This legislation, while it may reduce criminal activity on the web, enables a level of surveillance and censorship that would encourage one to explore a network like the anonymous web. Unfortunately, political division in the region, between competing Christian and Islamic forces, has led to terrorist activity that may incline these nations to pass rather stringent surveillance policy.

In late 2017, Nigeria experienced one of its broadest cases of web censorship when 21 websites associated with a separatist movement in the country were blocked. This sparked controversy about Internet rights in the country. New policy decisions were made in the ensuing months that affirmed the rights of citizens while also granting rights to the government for maintaining national defense.

East Africa

Policy and procedures regarding online privacy in East Africa vary widely from country to country, as does access to the Internet in general. Among most countries in the region, only about 40%–45% of adults use the Internet, compared to about 90% in the United States and other developed countries. The cost and inconsistency of Internet access has led some countries, like Uganda, to leave it largely unregulated. On the other hand, countries like Ethiopia have built fairly robust policy frameworks, which address the intrusion on privacy by ISPs and advertisers.

Zimbabwe represents a problematic strand of countries within this region. In 2002, Zimbabwe passed a piece of legislation entitled "Access to Information and Protection of Privacy Act" (Privacy International, 2016), which sounds promising but, unfortunately, is a misnomer. In reality, the law and those who execute it have severely hampered access to information through censorship tactics and spying on the communications of citizens.

Unfortunately, it is difficult to implement Tor in most East African countries. While Tor already takes a long time to retrieve information from servers, due to its complex routing systems described in the preceding chapters, the poor Internet infrastructure in East African countries often makes it impossible to connect.

South Africa

PRIVACY

The 1996 Constitution of South Africa, enacted following the end of the apartheid era in the country, provides extensive protections for data.

Specifically, Section 14 of the Constitution serves a similar role to the Fourth Amendment of the United States' Constitution (or, at least, in theory). It provides protection from unlawful search and seizure of property and the privacy of communications. The Protection of Personal Information Act of 2013 expands the powers of the government to preserve the privacy of citizens and organizations (Staunton et al., 2020). It established the position of Information Regulator, who is responsible for overseeing compliance to these laws. Given these protections, South Africa is much better off in terms of privacy than most countries on the African continent.

CENSORSHIP

Use of Tor in South Africa is legal, and there are several advocates active in the country who are actively educating the population about the value of the platform. However, attempts to integrate Tor into the offerings of libraries are limited, if they exist at all. Presently, there is opportunity for libraries to take a central role in cooperating with these advocate groups and introducing Tor to a broader population.

Brazil

PRIVACY

A right to privacy is provided in the constitution of Brazil (Viola de Azevedo Cunha and Itagiba, 2016). However, the infrastructure within the nation has historically let it susceptible to privacy infringement by various groups and other nations. Further, there are cases in which the nation itself appears to contradict its own policies. For instance, Brazil has surveillance laws that allow for telecommunications (including Internet use) to be intercepted for use in criminal investigations. Essentially, this authorizes a wire-tapping operation that may be used to monitor any individual suspected of a criminal activity. ISPs are also required to maintain logs of Internet connections, which contain sensitive data about web use behaviors. This data retention is designed to help in criminal investigations; however, it collects data on all users, not just known criminals. Additionally, social media interactions may be monitored by authorities, given any suspicion of criminal activity.

CENSORSHIP

Historically, Brazil has one of the largest pools of Tor users by sheer number; however, the rate of users per 100,000 people in the country in relatively meager compared to Europe, or even several other counties within South America (i.e., it has so many users because its population is so large, not because the technology has diffused thoroughly). Recent political change in Brazil, though, has correlated with a spike in Tor users. Presently, the use of Tor is not banned in Brazil, but attitudes toward surveillance within the nation present a potential challenge to the network. Libraries in Brazil that wish to provide enhanced privacy services may proceed with Tor, but should do so carefully, following the guidance of legal counsel.

Mexico

PRIVACY

Mexico's Constitution offers protections from government surveillance of data. Similar to the United States and many other nations worldwide, the law requires law enforcement to receive a warrant before interfering or intercepting the communications of private citizens. However, enforcement can be inconsistent and may not always extend to private organizations that collect data on users. Furthermore, a single ISP – Telmex, run by Carlos Slim, the fifth-wealthiest person in the world (as of late 2020) – has a virtual monopoly on all telecommunications in the country (Saenz-De-Miera-Berglind, Robles-Rovalo, and Morales-Contreras, 2017). The lack of competition gives Telmex the capacity to set some of its own rules as far as surveillance and Internet speeds.

CENSORSHIP

Tor is not directly blocked in Mexico, but many ISPs have, at times, restricted access to the platform, necessitating the use of bridges to access it. In the second half of the 2010s, Tor escalated its outreach to potential users and advocates in Mexico, including a two-day developers' event held in Mexico City in 2018. With its proximity to the United States and the Tor Project's creators, Mexico makes a logical option for the expansion of the Tor advocacy network.

Spain

PRIVACY

Though, as noted in the following subsection, censorship is a whole different matter, Spain has a fairly robust policy in terms of ensuring data privacy. The Spanish Constitution explicitly guarantees a right to privacy for citizens (Vilasau, 2004). At the turn of the new millennium, the country passed its first data privacy law, which has been revised several times over the years as technology and collection methods evolved. Spain's policy is very similar to other European countries. This is, in no small part, due to the strength of the European Union and its own directives, which will be discussed later in this chapter.

CENSORSHIP

The most pressing concern for Internet privacy in Spain is a fairly recent legislative order that allows the government broad discretion in blocking access to the web as it deems necessary to preserve "public health and safety." Certainly, even if its crafters were well-intentioned, it is unquestionable that this law infringes on citizens' rights. Further, laws pertaining to freedom of speech are some of the most restrictive among European countries. Websites pertaining to opposition political views and gender rights have frequently been blocked. So, even though the country has rather strict guidelines for data privacy among ISPs, there is ample concern for information privacy and access.

Tor has generally been legal to download and use in Spain since its inception. Given the nation's stance in support of data privacy, Tor may be seen as supporting its mission. In terms of the nation's history of censorship, Tor may be a valuable resource for circumventing the filtering of websites. Libraries should be careful when implementing Tor, based on the irascible viewpoints toward privacy within the country.

Italy

PRIVACY

While Italy has legislation in place to help assure online privacy, it also has relatively invasive data collection and storage laws (De Biasi, Mantovani, and Reggiani, 2020). ISPs in Italy are not only allowed but generally directed to store user data for years as part of national security efforts.

CENSORSHIP

Censorship is limited in the country but the use of Tor for preventing data collection is high. In fact, Italy has one of the greatest rates of Tor use per 100,000 Internet users in the world.

Why Fear Data Collection?

The purpose of online data collection by governments is for it to be used only in the circumstance in which it is needed as part of a criminal case. So why, if this is the case, would any law-abided citizen fear this data collection?

- It's YOUR data: It is the principle of the matter; your data should not be collected without your permission.
- Data breaches: Even in those circumstances in which data is treated with the upmost security, breaches are inevitable, particularly when the data at hand is incredibly valuable.

> • Support the protection of others' data: While data collection by a government may not put you directly at risk, vulnerable populations are at risk by government tracking. By opposing this tracking, you are protecting these populations as well.

Red Flag

China

PRIVACY

As opposed to the scattered legislation in some nations, like the United States, policy in China is much more centralized and cohesive. While the concept of privacy protection in relatively young in the country, its recent history, including the 2018 Standard for privacy, exceeds many of the provisions in U.S. law.

As is common in most data privacy law, the Standard stipulates that the collection of personal information must be consented to by the user before collection occurs (KPMG China, 2017). The statement associated with this consent must be clear enough to be reasonably understood by an average adult and must be descriptive of why and how data will be used. Anyone under the age of 14 is considered a minor and must have a parent's consent on their behalf. Data shared in a public forum is not held to the same standard and may be collected without consent (as is done in a lot of web-based research).

Organizations/services that collect user data must provide the following information to all users:

• How frequently will data be collected, and where will it be stored.
• The types of data will be secured and potential risks.
• Contact information for the data holder.

Data may only be transferred or shared if the holder has consent from the user or the data has been entirely de-identified. Additionally, the Standard sets requirements for organizations that handle large amounts of data to employ security teams.

In addition to the standard, which applies mainly to data collection by industry, a 2017 cybersecurity law provides guidance at a personal level. Under this law, data generated by "critical information infrastructure operators" must be stored domestically (in China). It limits collection of Chinese citizens' data by foreign organizations (certainly, having control of what sites citizens can access helps in this regard as well).

On the other hand, the law does not do much to protect citizens from surveillance by the country itself. It has been suggested that several thousand operators may be employed within the country with the purpose to monitor the usage of the Internet and communications on social media. This ties directly into the country's policies toward censorship.

CENSORSHIP

"The Great Firewall of China," as it has been termed, is used to restrict access to a wide number of websites and services – including Tor. Obviously, Tor's pro-information access agenda causes its supporters to be unwilling to accept this censorship. Therefore, researchers, developers, and just general supporters have worked tirelessly to circumvent the "Great Firewall," with a fair bit of success. For instance, several groups have studied how China manages to restrict Tor (generally, at the point where a computer initially attempts to connect to Tor – or form a "handshake"). Additionally, it appears that not all computers are barred from connecting, with Research universities, in particular, having the capacity to connect (it is worth noting that many Chinese Research Universities maintain Facebook, Twitter, and YouTube pages, among others, which are normally blocked within the country).

For the user who is willing to brave the risk, there are always a few ways to circumvent the censure. Mirror sites – an exact copy of a website that is posted at a different URL – can be used, at least temporarily, to outrace site filters. Often a mirror site may be posted, with the URL shared via social networks (not necessarily the digital networks, but rather real human connections). Bridges are used to connect users to the Tor network when it is censored in their country. Bridges are relays that are not listed in the public directory of Tor relays (and thus cannot be easily targeted by a country). Bridges may also incorporate additional layers of encryption to further obscure detection.

So there are ways for users in China to connect to Tor; however, it is unlikely that a library could manage (either practically or, certainly, lawfully) to operate on the Tor network. What these libraries might do is provide information to individual users that may support their use of anonymity platforms. Advocates from other countries may similarly work to educate their library colleagues in China and similar countries.

Iran

PRIVACY

Iran does not have any laws that specifically protect the privacy of its citizens. There are some privacy concepts built into certain cybercrime and criminal codes passed within the nation, but the extent to which these actually protect individuals within the country from surveillance by the country or other entities is likely limited. As with China, it is believed that surveillance by authorities within Iran may be a regular occurrence.

CENSORSHIP

Iran is perhaps the most restrictive of all countries in terms of Internet privacy and the use of Tor. According to a 2013 study by Aryan, Aryan, and Halderman, over one-fourth of surface websites are blocked in Iran at any given time, including half of the top 500 most-visited sites worldwide and particularly social media sites (Facebook, Twitter, and YouTube) and sites operated in Western countries or that provide broad information (Wikipedia, New York Times). Generally, access to Tor within the country is nearly impossible without the use of bridges. Anecdotally, in our experiences with colleagues from Iran, it is almost always necessary to share screenshots of content on webpages rather than simply sharing the URL. Many sites that one would not possible think to be restricted (such as the website of a smartwatch retailer) are completely blocked for Iranian users.

Russia

PRIVACY

Several pieces of legislation were passed in the middle years of the first decade of the 21st century that cover the usage of personal data collection from web users, direct marketing to users based on personal data, and storage of user data for extended periods of time (Lokot, 2020). These laws stipulate that consent must be received for the collection of data. Sensitive personal information – including racial demographics, political opinions, religious beliefs, health conditions, and sexual life – should generally be collected under no circumstances. Only relevant data should be collected. Data should be collected and stored only for the length of time necessary to perform the tasks stated in the user agreement. These policies, however, are not always enforced as well as the privacy-minded might wish. That is why, in 2017, the Russian President signed an amendment of the law that significantly increases the punishment for violations (increasing it by a factor of about ten).

CENSORSHIP

Russia has a *complicated* relationship with Tor. On the one hand, Tor has been used by the Russian government/military for a host of questionable operations (like influencing politics overseas). Russia is also known for providing asylum to Edward Snowden, an ardent supporter of Tor. On the other hand, Russia is responsible for possibly the most coordinated attempt to deanonymize the entire Tor network (BBC, 2019). One likely reason for this irascible behavior: The large number of average citizens in Russia who have been using Tor in recent years – the second most among all countries, averaging up to 400,000 users (17% of all users) a day in early 2020 (Tor Project, 2020) – suggesting an upswell of citizens who feel it necessary to bypass the government's web restrictions. The Russian government has even offered monetary rewards for strategies to take down Tor.

Targets of Censorship

In the Global North, or developed countries, we might think of censorship primarily being directed toward political dissention. However, much of the censorship on the web is not directed toward content that directly challenges a government (i.e., criticism of the CCP) but rather content that is considered socially impermissible. In many countries, this includes content that readers in the Global North would generally consider to be permissible, if not vital, such as support groups for LGBT youths, youths in gender transition, women's advocacy groups, religious groups. Generally, in Western Europe, Australia, Japan, and most of North and South America, homosexuality is accepted by the majority (if not large majority) of the population and gay marriage is legalized in many of them. This is not the case in other areas, where discussion of the topic of homosexuality is so discouraged that individuals from these countries may struggle to comprehend the concept of gender transition or gay marriage. In much of Africa, the Middle East, Asia, and Eastern Europe, homosexuality is highly discouraged or illegal, and possibly punishable by death. Websites that support LBGT individuals are often blocked in these countries.

Another common object of censorship that is widely accepted in most countries in the Global North is pornography. In some countries, all pornography is prohibited, in others only certain types of pornography may be prohibited. Some readers may say that it is all the better if pornography was banned everywhere; however, some of the most significant consequences of a complete prohibition of pornography can be the creation of a black market and an increase in demand for sex workers and sexual exploitation. This is seen in some countries with strict prohibition, such as Iran, India, China, and Northern Africa.

The censorship of these types of topics is what drives us, the authors, to support further development of anonymous web networks. We work with many excellent people from these high-censorship countries we discuss above, but we do not hold any punches when talking about what we see as serious flaws in their nations' governments (nor do we do so when criticizing our own government – and we do that a fair bit even in this book). It is important to be able to distinguish a nation's leadership from its people, certain beliefs and practices that seem objectively problematic to us from the cultural and societal structures in which they have become embedded in those countries – it is important, when talking about subjects like censorship, to respect the people and their values while also feeling comfortable in taking a firm stance that censorship is wrong and harsh punishments for activities that cause no harm to fellow human beings is wrong. We should engage in discourse about why we believe this is the case. We should support platforms like Tor that allow individuals in those countries to access the information they need.

How Has the Anonymous Web Been Used in Different Regions?

This section addresses two related questions. First, which countries use Tor the most and use bridges (to circumvent censorship) the most. Second, who and how do individuals and organizations within different parts of the world use the Tor network. In other words, the first question provides quantitative answers, while the second provides qualitative discussion.

Countries with the Most Tor Users

Figure 4.2 displays the top five countries by Tor users. The United States and Russia consistently swap the top and second spot. Over the three months displayed in this chart, the United States averaged 363,000 users per day, compared to 340,000 for Russia. In terms of number of Tor users per 1000 people in each country, Russia has the highest rate at 2.3 per 1000, followed by Germany at 2.1 per 1000, France at 1.3 per 1000, the United States at 1.1 per 1000, and the United Kingdom at 1.0 per 1000. Some of the highest rates per 1000 (though not by just raw number of users) are Israel at 1.3 users per 1000, Canada at 1.2 per 1000, Hong Kong at 0.9 per 1000, Denmark at 0.8 per 1000, and Australia at 0.8 per 1000.

Comparatively, Nigeria averages 0.008 users per 1000, South Africa has 0.08 users per 1000, China at 0.002 per 1000, Brazil at 0.2 per 1000, Mexico at 0.009 per 1000, Uganda at 0.01 per 1000, and Egypt at 0.02 per 1000. This

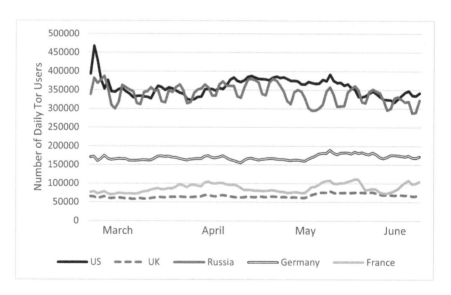

Figure 4.2 Five Countries with Most Tor Users

Source: Data from metrics.torproject.org, July 8, 2020.

demonstrates the discrepancy in the use of Tor between "developing" and "developed" countries. Both the infrastructure in place and the advocacy for the platform are limited in these countries.

Countries with the Most Tor Bridge Users

Tor "bridges" are used to access Tor in a country where the network is censored. Therefore, the bridge user statistics give a good indication of countries where potential Tor censorship is occurring. Here, we will focus just on the top four countries with the most bridge users. In Figure 4.3, the number of daily users from March 1 to June 1, 2020 is shown for the four countries with the most Tor bridge users. To make a fun guessing game out of it, the countries are labeled only as "Country X" (1-4). Below, we will reveal the name of each country in the chart and discuss their history with Tor censorship and bridges. Hint: Each of the four countries is discussed separately in the opening section of this chapter.

Country 1

Though country 1 has the fewest number of daily users among the four in this chart, many readers may have guessed this country to be that with the highest number of bridge users – if based on the sheer number of Internet users alone! The problem with that assumption is that this country (we might say, unfortunately) does a fairly successful job at quashing Tor.

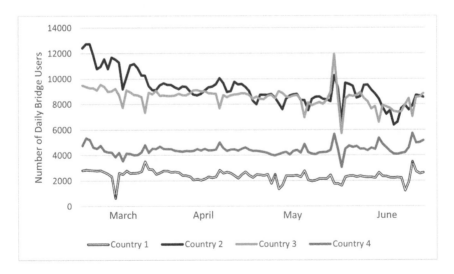

Figure 4.3 Four Countries with the Most Tor Bridge Users

Source: Data from metrics.torproject.org, July 8, 2020.

Country 2

This country makes it virtually impossible to access content not approved by government as "culturally appropriate." There is a significant vested interest among the government in controlling all information transfer to and from its citizens. At the same time, it is virtually impossible to access Tor in this country *unless* a bridge is used, as it is moderately successful at blocking the network.

Country 3

This country has a complicated relationship with Tor, which extends to its attempts both to use the platform for broad political gain and ban it for use by its own population. Country 3 is no stranger to controversy, invasion, and potentially illegal political activities on the web. This controversy often extends to its relationship with country 4.

Country 4

This country is yet another that has a love/hate relationship with Tor. To be fair (?), it just has a lot of users overall, so maybe this many bridge users is inevitable?

The Answers

Have you got your guesses ready? Well, let us see how you did.

All three of the countries we placed in the "red flag" subsection in the opening section of this chapter are among the four with most bridge users. Country 1 is actually China, with the fewest users of the four. Country 2 is Iran, which exhibits a bit of back-and-forth in terms of the most bridge users with country 3, Russia. Country 4 then, of course, is the United States.

Bridge Users Per 100,000

Among the countries shown in Figure 4.3, the United States has 1.4 users per 100,000, China has 0.2 per 100,000, Russia has 6.1 per 100,000, and Iran has 10.7 per 100,000. While Russia and Iran have, by far, the most bridge users, there are a few countries that have rates per 100,000 on part with the United States. Israel has a rate of 1.2 per 100,000, France has about 1.5 per 100,000, and the United Kingdom has about 1.7 per 100,000.

There are many countries that have few users of Tor and Tor bridges that might be considered the potential hotspots for use based on censorship activities. For instance, North Korea averages a handful of users per day and one bridge user and Syria averages about 400 users and two dozen bridge users. As discussed in the "Countries with the Most Tor Users" section, the challenge in this country is that the Internet in general is just not accessible to the population. In North Korea, connection to the Internet is severely limited among citizens, with most connections coming only via government and university servers.

Figure 4.4 displays the number of daily Tor bridge users worldwide from 2012 to 2020. Included in this data set are four clear "peaks," where the number of users, for about a five day period, were much higher than typical. Just for a frame of reference (not to imply causation), here are some of the events that happened on these dates: June 2015 – a series of terrorist attacks by ISIL/ISIS throughout the Middle East; March 2017 – United Kingdom officially announces Brexit negotiations; June 2018 – G7 Summit held in Canada; December 2019 – Russia banned from international sports for four years due to doping offenses. What is more important than the peaks (which may also be due to some data collection error or malfunctioning in the network) is the overall trend. If you smooth the jagged line shown in the chart, it is evident that the number of average daily users of Tor has increased from less than 10,000 in 2012–2015 to over 40,000 in 2017–2020. That is a four-fold increase over the period of roughly two years: 2015 and 2016.

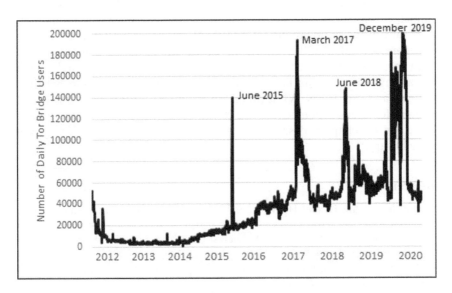

Figure 4.4 Tor Bridges: A Map of Censorship Activity

Source: Data from metrics.torproject.org, July 8, 2020.

Global Cooperation

This chapter demonstrates that online privacy and the use of Tor are world-wide issues. Virtually, all nations have some number of Tor users, and those that have only a few users are typically those that have only limited Internet access in general. While Tor is used more broadly and better understood by Internet users in developed countries in Europe and North America, there is clear need for this technology to be adopted in developing nations where threats related to censorship and surveillance are prevalent. Collaborative research and efforts to promote Tor as an information access resource for library and information organizations worldwide is needed. As with much research conducted today in librarianship, findings in one context, while not necessarily generalizable to all situations, can be useful in informing research and practice in other contexts. So, it is important that this research is shared in outlets that are accessible to professionals worldwide through global publishers or open access sources like *Information Technology and Libraries* journal published by the American Library Association.

Organizations like the International Federation of Library Associations (IFLA) can also be vital to improving cooperative efforts. These organizations are important disseminators of information and policy that impacts both developing and developed nations alike. Shared leadership from a variety of nations within these organizations also ensures that the ideas (like those discussed in this book) do not remain endemic to one nation but are broadly disseminated to thought leaders across the globe. So, while implementing Tor in your library is a nice step for your service population, advocacy at the national and international levels is what will truly lead to broader acceptance of the technology within and beyond the profession.

In the following two chapters, we will discuss the means through which the anonymous web can be integrated into library operations at both the systems and user levels. While all information up to this point is a valuable context for the acceptance and use of the anonymous web by individuals, these coming chapters describe how to implement a service like Tor within your library.

References

Aryan, S., Aryan, H. and Halderman, J. A. (2013), "Internet censorship in Iran: A first look", In *Proceedings of the 3rd USENIX Workshop on Free and Open Communication on the Internet.* Retrieved from https://www.jhalderm.com/pub/papers/iran-foci13.pdf

Bellon, A. (2021), "Drafting the digital republic law: Sociology of the political work of digital reformers", *Reseaux*, Vol. 225, No. 1, pp. 23–53.

Bischoff, P. (2020), Which countries have the worst (and best) cybersecurity? Retrieved from https://www.comparitech.com/blog/vpn-privacy/cybersecurity-by-country/

Brandeis, L. and Warren, S. (1890), "The right to privacy", *Harvard Law Review*, Vol. 4, No. 5, pp. 193–220.

British Broadcasting Company. (2019, July 22), *Russian intelligence 'targets Tor anonymous browser.'* https://www.bbc.com/news/technology-49071225/

De Biasi, F., Mantovani, A. and Reggiani, E. (2020), *Privacy in Italy*, Thomson Reuters, Toronto, CA.

James, M. C. (2013), "A comparative analysis of the right to privacy in the United States, Canada, and Europe", *Connecticut Journal of International Law*, Vol. 29, pp. 257–300.

Johnston, C. (2015, March 11), "Tor should not be banned in Britain", *The Guardian*. Https://www.theguardian.com/technology/2015/mar/11/tor-should-not-be-banned-in-britain

KPMG China. (2017, February), *Overview of China's cybersecurity law.* Retrieved from assets.kpmg/content/dam/kpmg/cn/pdf/en/2017/02/overview-of-cybersecurity-law.pdf

Library of Congress. (2020), *Online privacy law: Australia.* Retrieved from https://loc.gov/law/help/online-privacy-law/2017/australia.php

Lokot, T. (2020), "Data subjects vs. people's data: Competing discourses of privacy and power in modern Russia", *Media Communication*, Vol. 8, No. 2, pp. 314–322.

Macrina, A. and Phetteplace, E. (2015), "The Tor browser and intellectual freedom in the digital age", *Reference and User Services Quarterly*, Vol. 54, No. 4, pp. 17–20.

Nwankwo, I. S. (2016), "Information privacy in Nigeria", In Makulio, A. B., *African data privacy laws*, Springer, London, UK.

Privacy International. (2016), *The right to privacy in Zimbabwe.* Retrieved from hrp.law.harvard.edu/wp-content/uploads/2016/04/Zimbabwe_upr2016.pdf

Saenz-De-Miera-Berglind, O., Robles-Rovalo, A. and Morales-Contreras, R. (2017), "Review of the Mexican telecommunications market", *Journal of Telecommunications and the Digital Economy*, Vol. 5, No. 1, pp. 70–91.

Spencer, A. and Patel, S. (2019), "Applying the data protection act 2018 and general data protection regulation principles in healthcare settings", *Nursing Management*, Vol. 26, No. 1, pp. 34–40.

Staunton, C., Adams, R., Anderson, D., Croxton, T., Kamuya, D., Munene, M. and Swanepoel, C. (2020), "Protection of personal information act 2013 and data protection for health research in South Africa", *International Data Privacy Law*, Vol. 10, No. 2, pp. 160–179.

Tor Project. (2020, May 25), Metrics: Users. Retrieved from https://metrics.torproject.org/userstats-relay-table.html

Vilasau, M. (2004), The right to privacy and to personal data protection in Spanish legislation, https://www.uoc.edu/dt/eng/vilasau0904.pdf

Viola de Azevedo Cunha, M. and Itagiba, G. (2016), "Between privacy, freedom of information and freedom of expression: IS there are right to be forgotten in Brazil?", *Computer Law and Security Review*, Vol. 32, No. 4, pp. 634–641.

5   Integrating the Anonymous Web in Libraries and Information Organizations

Now that we have given you a firm understanding of what the anonymous web is, how it works, and what benefits it can give, it is time to start talking about how to integrate it into information organizations. What is involved? What types of access to the anonymous web should you offer? How do you prepare your organization and the people in it to provide this service?

Libraries and librarians, of course, love information and the access to it. We have always been leaders in providing access to as much of it as we can. We know that access can only come when we reject the barriers and censorship that certain powers feel entitled to place between us and the free flow of knowledge. Certain entities have determined that knowledge is dangerous and are, thus, inclined to limit access. The Internet, with its global reach and ever-expanding wealth of information, is hard to limit. Governments, organizations, and individuals around the world are constantly trying to control who can use the Internet, and what they can see on it.

Public libraries are in the ideal position to be a leader in providing information, training, and access to the anonymous web to a wide cross-section of people. Since public libraries exist in most communities, both large and small, rural and urban, they have tremendous reach and can tailor their services to the public they serve rather than relying on some carte-blanche policy or educational framework to work in all situations. In this chapter, we provide a general understanding of how anonymous web platforms – particularly Tor, since this platform is the most popular, extensible, and user-friendly – may be integrated into library services and become a priority in the advocacy and service goals of these organizations.

Integrating the Anonymous Web

How does a library or other information agency begin the process of implementing the anonymous web? What is involved in maintaining it?

Let us begin with some ideas of how a library or other information organization can utilize the anonymous web. The first obvious choice would be to offer one of the anonymous web platforms on publicly available computers. This can be done on computers inside the library and open to patrons, or in devices

DOI: 10.4324/9781003093732-6

that patrons can check out and take away from the library. It is also possible to allow the Internet connection for the library to be utilized by anonymous web applications as a part of the network. Finally, and most importantly, we believe, is the implementation of educational programs to patrons.

Since the anonymous web is not one single application, but rather a variety of different applications, each application must be evaluated to understand how they are used, and what it takes to implement them. Tor is the first choice that most libraries have turned to. This mostly due to the way that it connects to the anonymous web, its ability to host. onion sites only available to other Tor users, and its feature to allow Tor users to access the surface web with a high degree of protection.

To start with, any organization interested in implementing the anonymous web must fully understand it with education. Using online resources mentioned in this book, begin to research the anonymous web and how it works. Then using the information in Chapter 6, prepare a basic education plan for staff.

An education plan for library staff should focus not necessarily the how of the anonymous web, but more on the why. Some staff may want to know more about the inner details of how Tor routing works, or how a VPN protects privacy. Every staff member should understand:

• Public libraries and their role in protecting privacy for their patrons.
• Any relevant library policies as they relate to privacy and security for patrons.
• All applicable local, state, and federal laws as they relate to patron privacy.
• Dispel any myths about the anonymous web, and what it can do.
• Simple starting places for staff to introduce to patrons.

Information on public libraries roles in protecting patron privacy can come from many sources including this book, other books on the topic (see Chapter 6 for more details), and professional organizations. The American Library Association has an entire site devoted to understanding the role of public libraries in privacy – Choose Privacy Everyday (https://chooseprivacyeveryday.org/).

Information for the public can come in many forms. It can be as simple as a quick pamphlet on privacy available at the public computers or other areas of the library that includes information on how the library protects the privacy of their users, and what they can do to help. Patron education can also come in the format of a series of informational classes on the Internet, the anonymous web, how privacy is lost, and what the library is doing to protect it. The easiest and most efficient form of patron education comes from an educated staff. For a staff member to be able to explain one-on-one with a patron how privacy is lost, and what the library is doing to protect it shows the commitment the library has made to understand privacy.

Offering Tor

The easiest way to start integrating the anonymous web in a library is to offer the Tor browser. Most libraries offer some form of Internet access to their patrons, either in freestanding computers that are available on demand, or to laptops that can be checked out and used in the library or at home. Taking the installation files from the Tor project website located at https://www.torproject.org/download/, such as in Figure 5.1, can be installed on almost any Windows, MAC, Linux, or Android device. Once it is installed, an icon placed on the desktop will open an encrypted connection using the library Internet service to the Tor network. It is important to make sure that the Tor browser bundle is kept up to date. They release updates and patches to the Tor browser to maintain the security of the application.

Creating an Onion Site

Another interesting way for a library to become involved in the anonymous web, especially using Tor is to publish their web services on the Tor network. Remember back when we talked about Tor and how it works. Even though Tor is great at allowing people to access the surface web with a higher degree of privacy and security, there are also sites only available on the network. These sites are called onion sites, and anyone, including a library, can publish their own information to an onion site. This is done using what is called onion services by the Tor project.

Onion services sites work differently from regular surface Internet sites. Most Internet sites are given an IP address which is publicly available. They utilize special look-up servers called Domain Name Servers or DNS servers that associate domain names (like Google.com) with an IP address. When your computer wants to find Google.com, it requests the IP address from

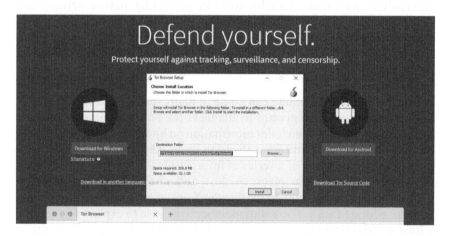

Figure 5.1 Tor Project Download Interface

a DNS server. Once it knows what the IP address is, it connects to the website and starts talking. Since the Tor network is designed to create anonymity to the users and the people who publish information, a different method was designed to hide the IP address of the server. This process uses the onion service protocol to advertise onion sites to the network without revealing their IP address. When a new onion site enters the Tor network, it searches for relays and asks them to introduce it on the network. When the relays do these types of introductions, they do so without giving out any information about the host. They act as anonymizing circuits. When there are several relays that have become anonymizing circuits for a site, the onion service creates an onion service descriptor. The descriptor is a list of a site's introduction points and is used to create an identity key pair. The identity key pair consists of two keys – a private key and a public key. The private key is used to encrypt the onion service descriptor and the public key becomes the onion service address (remember what onion sites addresses look like? The onion address for the Tor Project website is: http://2gzyxa5ihm7nsgg-fxnu52rck2vv4rvmdlkiu3zzui5du4xyclen53wid.onion/). The public key for the site's service descriptor is part of that address. If your computer is on the Tor network, and you wanted to connect to the Tor project website, your browser would use the site address and use it to verify the encryption on the service descriptor and use it to find the introduction points for the site. Your computer connects to one of the introduction point relays and asks it to become a rendezvous point. That relay then becomes the "middle man" in the communication between your computer and the Tor project website. It handles all the traffic between them so neither side is aware of who the other really is. All this communication between your computer, the Tor network, the introduction points, and the Tor Project website is done with end-to-end encryption, and anonymized as much as possible.

The full details and process to create an onion site are beyond the scope of this book, but a great place to start is the Tor project community site located at https://community.torproject.org/onion-services/. To give you a basic understanding of the process, it can be simplified down to a few steps. First, install a web service application like Apache or Nginx and put your website contents on it. Then, you install the Tor onion service software on the same server, and configure it to see the contents of your website. Once it is configured to see your site, simply restarting the Tor service software will get the process started and your site is on the Tor network. Once up and running, there are other optional steps a site can take to provide more security for themselves, and to create more privacy.

Does a library or other information agency really need to put their website on the Tor network and take all these steps to ensure their privacy? Maybe not, but the practice of doing so is a great way to advocate for the use of the anonymous web, and to help promote its use. It helps library staff to understand how it works and creates opportunities to educate patrons (Figure 5.2).

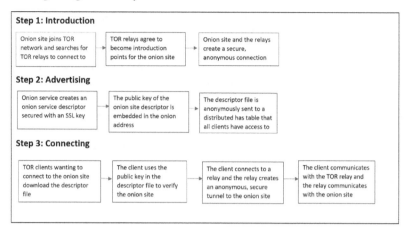

Figure 5.2 The Onion Service

Becoming a Tor Relay

One of the best ways a library can become involved in providing anonymous web access to users is by becoming a Tor relay. As mentioned earlier, the Library Freedom Project is working hard to promote the use of Tor in public libraries, but also to promote the creation of Tor relays in public libraries (Macrina, 2016). By doing this, libraries can become the backbone of a distributed network of sustained, protected relays that keep the Tor network running the way it should be.

Refer back in this book to the chapter on how the Tor network works. It uses nodes or relays that help to route packets through the network. These relays encrypt and decrypt data as it passes through. Relays are not always secure though. Remember the discussion on how relays can be compromised? A nefarious person or organization can create an exit relay that captures all the traffic passing through it to the surface web. Of course, this data is mostly (or should be) encrypted and difficult to read. Usage of other tools like HTTPS everywhere will help to make this more difficult.

Also, not all relays on the Tor network are the most efficient. The network does a great job of creating routes that utilize fast, low latency connections, but not all of them are. Relays can become slow, or suddenly drop from the network causing re-routing issues and delays. Having relays that are fast, reliable, and safe make the entire network strong.

To get started becoming a relay, start by reading up on the whole process, what is involved, and what to install. The Tor project of course has a wealth of articles on how to install Tor as a relay. You can start with their most recent Guide to Running a Tor Relay (https://blog.torproject.org/new-guide-running-tor-relay), or their community page on running a Tor relay (https://community.torproject.org/relay/).

There are three basic types of nodes on a Tor relay (Haraty and Zantout, 2014). A guard or non-exiting relay is a fast relay on the network that does not provide any kind of exit off the network, just a way to move between different relays on the network. If a guard relay is not fast enough, it will be demoted to a simple middle relay. Guard and middle relays are the simplest type of relay to run since they do not require a lot of setup or configuration. Also, since they are not the originators of traffic, and do not provide an exit to the surface web, they typically do not see a lot of complaints or abuse complaints from other operators. They just pass the traffic.

Exit relays are the final step in the relay chain for the Tor network. They accept packets from the middle or guard relays and direct it to the surface web for delivery. Of all the relay types, exit relays are the most likely to be targeted for legal and liability reasons. Since the traffic exiting the Tor network appears to be coming from the exit relay, legal agencies and copyright holders tend to believe that the relay hosting agency is responsible.

The third type of relay is a bridge. A bridge relay is a specialized relay that can be used by individuals or organizations who need an extra layer of protection when connecting to the Tor network. When a relay is created on the Tor network, it advertises itself to the network and is publicly visible. The IP address of the Tor relay is visible, so the hosting agency or location is known. Bridge relay's, however, do not publish themselves on the public Tor directory, so are more likely to not be blacklisted or blocked by governments or agencies who wish to block access to the Tor network. If you were an oppressive government and you were trying to prevent your people from being able to get out on the public Internet and tell the world how bad things are in your country, you would find it easy to get a listing of all the publicly advertised Tor relays and block them with a national firewall (Winter and Lindskog, 2012). Then you just sit back and relax believing you have stopped the voices of dissent in your country from broadcasting the truth. Well, the Tor bridge will allow them to connect and speak to the world.

Becoming a Tor relay does have certain requirements that must be met. You must be able to provide enough bandwidth to handle the traffic that passes through it. You can control the amount of traffic, and adjust it as needed but to become a useful part of the network, it is best to give as much as possible without affecting your regular Internet use. A typical Tor relay will need to accept somewhere around 7000 concurrent connections. This amount of simultaneous connections would overwhelm a standard, home router. You must be able to provide an Internet router that can handle that number and higher of connections. A good starting point for Tor relays in regard to bandwidth is around 16 Mbps upload and 16 Mbps download speed. Most consumer connections nowadays start out at 3–4 times faster than that. Commercial or business class Internet will most likely be able to handle these speeds, but it would not hurt to double check before you start. The amount of traffic passing through a relay is also a consideration. The Tor network requires that the relay be able to handle at a minimum

100 GB of incoming traffic and 100 GB of outgoing traffic a month. A public IP address is also required. Ideally, it would be best if the IP address was a static address, and not dynamic. If the IP address is not static, then the relay's publicly advertised address would be constantly changing, and causing routes to change, and relay databases to be constantly updated. Although a static IP is not required, it is highly recommended in order to keep the updates and changes necessary to a minimum. Of course, the server you have on your network running the Tor relay software must be able to meet certainly minimum requirements. Tor asks that it:

- Has at least 512 MB of RAM (exit relays should have 1.5 GB).
- Have some disk storage, but not much. Around 200–300 MB is fine.
- Be running a CPU that was developed in the last 10 years.
- Stay up and running as much as possible. Relays are not required to be up all the time, but the more the better (Tor Project, 2021).

There are other considerations that must be considered before turning on the relay. Your Internet host must be aware of what you are doing. When you start up your Tor relay, you will start taking in and sending out a lot of traffic. This sudden change could appear to be some kind of attack or infection to your provider. They might shut down or throttle your Internet to protect you. If you are considering creating an exit relay, it would be best to have a discussion with your provider to make sure they understand the potential risks. Once again, it is possible that exit relays may appear to be allowing copyright infringement or illegal activities. It is likely that your Internet provider could receive these notices as well. Talk to your provider to make sure they understand what a Tor relay is, and how it works. It might also help to talk them about a custom WHOIS record. A WHOIS record is simply an informational tool for IP addresses. For example, if you were to look up the WHOIS record for the public IP address of the American Library Association website (currently, it is 173.237.139.43), it will return the name, address, and phone number for the company that hosts the ALA website (currently, it is Tierpoint LLC). If someone were to do a WHOIS lookup on your public Tor relay IP address, it would return your Internet provider. You can alleviate their worries by creating a custom WHOIS record that points to you instead of them.

The Tor project website has complete instructions on creating, configuring, and managing a Tor relay on your network. You can also find more instructional guides on the Internet on using the Tor software. The Library Freedom Project has a great page for librarians on all kinds of Tor and privacy-related topics at https://libraryfreedom.org/privacy-toolkit-for-librarians/.

One of the newer relay options is Snowflake. Snowflake is an easier-to-run proxy on the Tor network that is particularly designed to support the circumvention of censorship. Unlike some other types of relays, Snowflake relays do not require a relay to be operational 24/7. It can be downloaded as an extension on a Firefox or Chrome browser that operates when your computer is in use and allows you to continue to use the Internet normally while allowing individuals in high-censorship areas to connect securely to the Tor network. According to a 2021 survey by Tor, the countries with the most Snowflake users include the United States, Germany, Spain, Russia, China, and Iran (Cohosh, 2021). Operating computers as Snowflake relays, using the Chrome or Firefox extension, may be a welcome idea for some libraries that do not wish to dive all the way into the rabbit-hole of anonymous web network relays but nonetheless want to help.

Rewarding Tor Relays?: An Interesting But Unlikely Idea

Biryukov and Pustograv (2015) discuss the potential to, essentially, use a cryptocurrency in order to pay Tor relays for their services. Such a scheme could work in several ways. One would be to have a cryptocurrency native to Tor (one that the Project itself creates), which can be sent to relays as long as they are operational (for instance, 0.0001 Tor Coin for each second that the relay is operating). The other would be for the Tor users to pay the compensation for the relays, like they do to their Internet service providers (you put an amount of cryptocurrency into an account and then that is automatically paid out to the relays at a rate of .0001, or something, per second). The second option is not viable, as it excludes many of the individuals who need Tor the most due to a lack of sufficient funding. The first option is compelling, especially considering the boom in cryptocurrency, but also faces its own challenges, including potential risks in compromising privacy, opening Tor up to potential legal and financial problems (dealing with taxation, legality of crypto), and a lack of interest/time available to dedicate to such a project. Most Tor relays serve that role not to gain anything other than pride that they are contributing to free, uncensored access to information.

Other Anonymous Web Tools

We spend a lot of time in this book and especially in this chapter talking about Tor. It is the most widely used anonymous web platform, but do not forget there are more. You can offer the Invisible Internet Project (I2P) and Freenet as well. Both I2P and Freenet are simple installs and can be put on public computers easily. The difference between them and Tor comes in the use. Tor comes bundled with a browser that is preconfigured to use the Tor network. I2P and Freenet, once installed and started, do not. The instead create the connection in the background which you can use other apps to use. It is recommended that for Freenet and I2P, you create a shortcut to a browser like Firefox that is already configured to use all the privacy settings recommended. For example, with Firefox, you can create a profile for the public computers that have the following settings that work with I2P:

- General, network settings – Set this to connect to a proxy. Create a manual proxy configuration for HTTP and HTTPS to 127.0.0.1 with a port number of 4444.
- Privacy and Security – Set the browser privacy to strict or custom settings.

Once this profile is created, an icon on the desktop can be created to use that profile. Freenet operates a similar way. A profile can be created using a browser like Firefox that has similar settings as I2P, but instead of setting a proxy to connect to the network, just change the homepage to point to: http://127.0.0.1:8888. Once that profile is created, an icon on the desktop can be created that points to it.

Of course, the biggest benefit of I2P and Freenet is that they mostly operate on their own networks, and mostly do not connect to the surface web. Once they are installed on a computer, a variety of other applications can be installed to use the networks. It is common to use IRC or chat applications, file sharing applications like BitTorrent, coding or programming applications, and many others. For a public computer in a library, a folder could be created that contains links to the various apps for each of the anonymous web networks.

Unlike Tor, there are no separate applications to run to integrate the library Internet connection into the I2P and Freenet networks. They both operate similar in that they use nodes to create the network. Once a computer starts up the I2P and Freenet software, they become a part of the network and start advertising themselves and passing traffic. There are ways to configure them on the computers to minimize the impact on the network and the Internet connection as a whole.

It is our recommendation that if you are considering integrating the anonymous web in your organization, start with Tor. It is the easiest to implement since it only requires a browser and application to be run to connect to the network and allows easy access to surface web information. For most patrons, this is the most likely use of the anonymous web. The other two networks, I2P and Freenet are more complicated to use since they run as services on the computer all the time and require specialized configuration or applications to access them. They mostly do not by default connect to surface web sites, so they are very specific in their use. Once the library is familiar with Tor, the board, staff, and patrons are used to it, then explore other options. Start running a Tor router. Create a couple of public computers that cater to Freenet and I2P with information with them on what they are and how they work.

Alternatives to the Anonymous Web: Are They Good Enough?

One thing that some libraries may propose/consider is offering some alternative to Tor, like DuckDuckGo or Brave. While these tools can be useful in certain instance and should be offered by libraries on their computers in addition to Tor, they are no alternative. As discussed in Chapter 2, DuckDuckGo is a search engine, like Google, not a web browser. It protects you while searching but does not offer privacy on external sites once you click on a link and are transported away. DuckDuckGo can be useful for mitigating the impact of filter bubbles – the effect where search engines "refine" search results based on past user behavior – however, the search engine has little control over external sites. Brave browser is a secure web browser that operates not by anonymous web networking but by automatically enabling all of the optional security/privacy features that are available on other browsers: Ad blockers, HTTPS Everywhere, and third-party cookies blocker.

While both DuckDuckGo and Brave have considerable value they are not, by any means, the "same thing" as Tor. Even with the built in privacy features of these platforms, they are more vulnerable to breaches of privacy. They are not autonomous networks. They still operate using the same networking principles as Google and Google Chrome. They have no means by which to circumvent censorship. They were created and are managed by corporations (Brave Software, Inc. and Duck Duck Go, Inc.), whereas Tor was created and managed by a U.S.-recognized non-profit organization (The Tor Project). It is advisable to offer access to all three platforms and allow users to decide which, if any, they wish to use.

Anonymous Web and Library Policy

In a 2021 article, we use existing public library mission and vision statements to help make a justification for the use of Tor within these organizations (Lund and Beckstrom, 2021). There is already a lot in library missions and policies that supports the use of the anonymous web. In the study, we examined the statements for 20 large public libraries in the United States: Those located in the ten most "liberal" cities in the United States (according to Tausanovitch and Warshaw, 2014) and the ten most "conservative" cities, in order to mitigate the potential for municipal influence on library policy. Among the 20 library policies, there were 31 identified references to the mandate of the library to provide "free and open access to information," which can only be done when patrons are free of censorship. There were 18 references to the library's duty to "maintain privacy and intellectual freedom of patrons," which, can only be accomplished if patrons have access to privacy platforms like Tor. There were also several references to the importance of free expression and exposure to diverse, research-based ideas. We believe that this language in the libraries' policies clearly shows that Tor aligns with the mission of libraries and, thus, should be a fundamental service to which all patrons have access.

We do, however, recommend that some policies should be revised in other areas in order to support the usage of Tor and other anonymous web platforms. For instance, many libraries in the United States outline strict filtering policies for all library computers (Lund, 2021a). While it is true that, to receive discounted Internet services in the United States, public libraries must filter certain content for children (which could potentially bar access to Tor, since it is not really possible to restrict access to certain sites), this restriction does not apply to adults or individuals with bona fide research needs. The implementation of a carte-blanche policy seems to be done out of laziness than anything else – it is easier to say, "all Internet access will be filtered," than to have separate policies for children and adults – as few libraries add any nuance to this policy and instead assume that all patrons should accept this policy because "it is the law," even though it is not actually what the law says. It is possible to have a set of policies for young users and another for mature users and, frankly, not doing so kind of makes it seem like you are okay with treating all patrons like children. Adults should be held responsible for what content they access. If they are caught accessing illegal content, they should be persecuted according to local and federal law, but they should be trusted to the computers lawfully – at least until it has been shown that they can no longer be trusted.

Many Internet use policies and user responsibility policies mention the collection of user information for specific purposes. For example, it is common for libraries to keep statistics of what computers are used in the library, and what applications are used on the computers. This is useful for libraries to understand the usage of the computers, and how they are used to create better services for their patrons (though it can, nonetheless, raise privacy concerns). Obviously, the use of a public computer and the use of the Tor browser on the computer could be used to identify who used the computer at that time. It is important, if usage data is collected for library purposes, for the library's policies to separate the usage of a public computer and its software from the user who used it. It may be useful – from many perspectives, including administrative and financial – to know that computer 13 was used by a patron from 2 to 3 PM, but the data should not be recorded as "Mike Fakename used computer 13 from 2 to 3 PM."

Here is an example policy statement for a library that offers access to Tor. Note that it is succinct, designed to state what is necessary and leave the rest for other documents (like the FAQs discussed shortly) or for employees to answer if a patron is interested.

"ABC Public Library is proud to provide access to the Tor browser, a unique, secure web browser. Patrons can use the Tor browser to access all the same web content they access on any other browser, and will benefit from enhanced privacy, as the browser will block web trackers and enable an anonymous web experience. The Tor browser can be accessed on all adult-use computers within the library. Any patrons with questions about the browser are encouraged to refer to the FAQ documents in the adult-use computer area or ask any library employee."

It is also important, of course, to have a policy in place in the case that the use of Tor gets challenged. We mentioned, with the case of Kilton Public Library in New Hampshire, that one of the strongest challengers of Tor may be law enforcement. Law enforcement can be very persuasive/intimidating if library employees are not prepared to respond. Library policies regarding Tor challenges should be similar to their policies regarding challenged books. In most cases, that means that someone desiring to challenging the platform needs to file a written complaint, which can then be considered by the library board. The responsibility for making decisions regarding Tor should be completely removed from any one library employee, not only because they may make a decision that the rest of the library staff disagrees with, but because that is simply a lot of responsibility to place on any one person.

In addition to clear policy, a frequently asked questions (FAQ) document is useful for patrons to have access to regarding the anonymous web and public computers. It is an efficient way to answer questions that patrons may be thinking about the anonymous web. It would be simple to create this FAQ in a Microsoft Word document and then print it out and tape it up behind the computers and/or offer it in the policies page on the library's website. Some sample questions and answers that might be included in this FAQ include:

- Why is the library offering anonymous web tools (Tor, etc.) for the public to use?
  - Public libraries are defenders of intellectual freedom, and the right of every user to pursue knowledge or information on any topic without fear of monitoring or judgment. The library has determined that the Internet is not always a place where individual research can be performed without government or commercial entities involving themselves. Offering anonymous web services provides library patrons with a higher level of privacy.
- Why does the library offer a service that is used to commit illegal acts?
  - The anonymous web can be used by criminals to commit illegal acts, but so does every other Internet access tool available. There are many other ways open to those who would commit crimes to become anonymous on the Internet besides the tools provided by the library.
- Is the anonymous web safe for teens and children?
  - Yes, it is. It operates and functions just like a regular Internet browser and does not explicitly provide access to inappropriate sites or content. Anyone using the anonymous web to access the Internet is just doing it in a way that provides an extra layer of privacy than regular access.
- Is this the only way the library provides privacy to Internet users?

- No, the library provides many other layers of privacy and security for library patrons. By using any of the computers in the library, a certain level of privacy is granted. Every computer is refreshed every day to remove any personal content, and all records of usage are cleared weekly. For more information regarding the privacy and security the library provides to their users, please refer to the library policies.

This by no means is a complete list of possible questions, but it gets you started. As time progresses, and you start exploring the implementation of more Anonymous web applications, and expanding the offerings, more questions will pop up. Take the time to ask your patrons and staff what works, and what does not. It will allow you to keep the applications relevant and keep staff educated on their use. Make sure you stay up to date with the various applications, and their changes. Stay in contact with other libraries and organizations that are using the Anonymous web so you can share ideas and develop solutions collaboratively.

References

Biryukov, A. and Pustograv, I. (2015), "Proof-of-work as anonymous micropayment: Rewarding a Tor relay", *International Conference on Financial Cryptography and Data Security, 2015*, pp. 445–455.

Cohosh. (2021), Snowflake moving to stable in Tor browser 10.5. Retrieved from https://blog.torproject.org/snowflake-in-tor-browser-stable

Haraty, R. A. and Zantout, B. (2014), "The Tor data communication system", *Journal of Communications and Networks*, Vol. 16, No. 4, pp. 415–420.

Lund, B. D. (2021a), "Public libraries' data privacy policies: A content and cluster analysis", *Serials Librarian*. Retrieved from https://doi.org/10.1080/03615 26X.2021.1875958

Lund, B. D. (2021b), "The Brave browser: A monetary opportunity for libraries in the cryptoverse", *Library Hi-Tech News*. Retrieved from https://doi.org/10.1108/LHTN-05-2021-0023

Lund, B. D. and Beckstrom, M. (2021), "The integration of Tor into library services: An appeal to the core mission and values of libraries", *Public Library Quarterly*, Vol. 40, No. 1, pp. 60–76.

Macrina, A. (2016), Tor at the heart: Library Freedom Project. Retrieved from https://blog.torproject.org/comment/225128

Tausanovitch, C. and Warshaw, C. (2014), "Representation in municipal government", *American Political Science Review*, Vol. 108, No. 3, pp. 605–641.

Tor, Project. (2021, September 4), *Relay requirements*. Retrieved from community.torproject.org/relay/relays-requirements/

Winter, P. and Lindskog, S. (2012), "How the great firewall of China is blocking Tor", In *Free and Open Communications on the Internet*, USENIX Association, Berkeley, CA.

6 Anonymous Web Education

There are not a lot of courses on the anonymous web available today. However, this is an emerging area of interest within some disciplines, as indicated by Belshaw et al. (2020). In this article, the authors describe a course within the criminal justice department at the University of North Texas, by the name of "Illicit Drugs and the Dark Web." This is certainly not the type of class we are advocating for in this book – but it is something nonetheless. The authors of this article provide a syllabus for this course, which makes evident that the true focus of the content is the Silk Road, rather than a holistic assessment of the anonymous web.

There are also a few courses out in the world of academia that may incorporate a lesson or module about the anonymous web. This is the case at Emporia State University, where the Library and Information Science (LIS) program's information technology course includes a module with content on the topic. The purpose of this module is not to teach how the anonymous web works or what. onion sites are; rather, the module just introduces the topic on a very basic level, to advocate that students research further. Not to toot our own horn too much, but we have built up a nice repertoire of practitioner-focused resources that can be used for a similar module, either in a library school course or in information literacy courses offered by academic libraries:

- Lund, Brady. 2019. The dark web for all! Journal of Information Ethics, 28(2), 109–116.
- Lund, Brady and Matt Beckstrom. 2019. The integration of Tor into library services. Public Library Quarterly, https://doi.org/10.1080/0161 6846.2019.1696078
- Lund, Brady. 2019. Using the dark web in libraries. https://web. archive.org/web/20200225164952/https://www.libraryjournal. com/?detailStory=Using-the-Dark-Web-in-Libraries-Field-Reports
- Smith, Carrie. 2019, June 24. In the deep beneath the iceberg. https:// web.archive.org/web/20190628121537/https://americanlibrariesmaga-zine.org/blogs/the-scoop/deep-beneath-iceberg/

DOI: 10.4324/9781003093732-7

However, one-off modules like the one we discuss here are not really the focus of this chapter. Rather, we are interested in classes that provide instruction to library patrons on how to use the anonymous web during their own browsing sessions. Fortunately, as we have discussed in the preceding chapters, there is minimal learning curve for the most popular anonymous web platform (Tor). Nonetheless, a few elements like advanced security settings and practices will require some training. Additionally, we want to discuss those platforms that have a little steeper learning curve and strategies to flatten that curve.

We will also discuss how a more advanced, semester-long graduate-level course in information science programs could cover the anonymous web, offering suggested learning outcomes and syllabus. We do this not only because it is a fun exercise (it is) but to counter the North Texas course that emphasizes only the criminal elements of this platform. We want to propose a course that blends library science and information systems concepts in a way that is fitting for the modern LIS program.

Should We Prepare for Controversy?

Certainly, offering a course on "How to use the anonymous web" is a pretty bold statement of your organization's perspective on the matter. So maybe it does not seem too irrational to think that your library could receive some backlash for offering such a class. In our experience as pre-senters on the anonymous web, we have received no serious backlash (in fact, quite the opposite). However, we are also presenting to librarians and library school students, not library patrons. So, it does seem prudent to have some plan in place in case this backlash is received. Fortunately, libraries are no strangers to preparing for potential controversy. One of the tremendous strengths of the profession is its network of powerful advocates.

One-Off Lessons

Perhaps the greatest challenge when teaching a class for a general group of patrons is that you cannot really make an assumption about their prior knowledge level. Particularly in public libraries, you may have vast discrepancies in computer literacy from patron to patron. Understanding the audience – gauging their technical knowledge of computers – is key to determining the extent of "systems" talk to include in your lesson (or if it is best to just teach basic install and use). Regardless, it is probably wise to enter any lesson with extensive knowledge yourself, rather than go in assuming you will be able to pull things together as you go. There are always a few very tech-savvy people in the audience that will want to pry for more detailed information about the platform – so while you might provide a lesson that focuses on the basic of Tor as a web browser, you should know the basics of the workings of the platform (that we provide in this book).

An important part of such a lesson, regardless of the specific content, is dispelling misinformation and exaggeration about the platform. As we do in this book, it is important to acknowledge the history of the anonymous web in a frank manner while also emphasizing the benefits of the technology. Allow the audience to form its own opinions about the platforms. There are several good alternatives to the anonymous web that individuals may consider if they are not comfortable with the platform.

You might also consider incorporating the anonymous web as just one aspect of a course on online searching or privacy practices. This strategy is commonly used by use when we present at conferences. While the anonymous web is interesting and potentially very useful, audiences tend to want to know about a variety of technologies, including browsers like Brave and search engines like DuckDuckGo that promote privacy, that are a little less controversial. So, the name of the session may be something along the lines of "Protecting Your Privacy Online" or "Safely Using the Library's Computers," and incorporate a variety of content.

Example Class

This section focuses on how a graduate-level course on the anonymous web, and related topics in information access and privacy, could be designed for information science programs, including an example syllabus.

Teaching in this class can incorporate many of the strategies and analogies we used earlier in this book, like the nested box analogies for Tor, I2P, and Freenet.

Example Syllabus:

Information Access, Privacy, and the Anonymous Web

Textbook: (You Are Reading It)

Course Learning Outcomes:

- Following this course, students will be able to:
    - Describe the basic threats to online privacy that exist on the Internet today
    - Identify basic concepts and terminology related to web-based systems and information privacy
    - Justify the need for enhanced privacy in library and information organizations
    - Apply knowledge of online privacy and the anonymous web to educate patrons of library and information organizations

Tentative Class Schedule:

Week	Readings	Assignments
Week 1: How the Internet works	Leiner, Barry M., Vinton G. Cerf, David D. Clark, Robert E. Kahn, Leonard Kleinrock, Daniel C. Lynch, Jon Postel, Larry G. Roberts, and Stephen Wolff. "A brief history of the Internet." ACM SIGCOMM Computer Communication Review 39, no. 5 (2009): 22–31; Lund and Beckstrom, Chapter 1	Discussion post #1
Week 2: Filter bubbles	Flaxman, Seth, Sharad Goel, and Justin M. Rao. "Filter bubbles, echo chambers, and online news consumption." Public Opinion Quarterly 80, no. S1 (2016): 298–320	Discussion post #2
Week 3: The need for online privacy	Bowers, Stacey L. "Privacy and library records." The Journal of Academic Librarianship 32, no. 4 (2006): 377–383; Clarke, Roger. "Internet privacy concerns confirm the case for intervention." Communications of the ACM 42, no. 2 (1999): 60–67; Lund and Beckstrom, Chapter 3	Discussion post #3
Week 4: VPNs and secure browsing	No reading	Students-as-teachers assignment
Week 5: Introduction to anonymous web platforms	About Tor (https://www.torproject.org/about/history/); Misata, Kelley. "the tor project: An inside view." *XRDS: Crossroads, The ACM Magazine for Students* 20, no. 1 (2013): 45–47	Discussion post #4
Week 6: How the anonymous web works	Goldschlag, David, Michael Reed, and Paul Syverson. "Onion routing." Communications of the ACM 42, no. 2 (1999): 39–41; Lund and Beckstrom, Chapter 2	Discussion post #5
Week 7: How the anonymous web is used	Macrina, Alison. "The Tor browser and intellectual freedom in the digital age." Reference & User Services Quarterly 54, no. 4 (2015): 17–20; Fabian, Benjamin, Florian Goertz, Steffen Kunz, Sebastian Müller, and Mathias Nitzsche. "Privately waiting–a usability analysis of the tor anonymity network." In *SIGeBIZ track of the Americas Conference on Information Systems*, pp. 63–75. Springer, Berlin, Heidelberg, 2010	Midterm assignment due Friday, 11:59PM

(Continued)

Week 8: Legal and criminal issues with the anonymous web	Ghappour, Ahmed. "Searching places unknown: Law enforcement jurisdiction on the dark web." Stan. Law Review 69 (2017): 1075–1136	Discussion post #6
Weeks 9 and 10: Integrating the anonymous web in information organizations	Lund, Brady, and Matt Beckstrom. "The Integration of Tor into Library Services: An Appeal to the Core Mission and Values of Libraries." Public Library Quarterly (2019): 1–17; Lund and Beckstrom, Chapter 5	Discussion post #7
Weeks 11 and 12: Educating others about the anonymous web	Lund and Beckstrom, Chapter 6	Discussion post #8
Weeks 13 and 14: Final project		Final project due Friday, 11:59PM

Assignments: (Further Instructions Are Provided in Course Modules)

Class Discussion Boards (10 points each):

One discussion board per module. Instructions for each discussion board assignment will be listed in the initial board post.

Students-as-Teachers Assignment (20 points):

Students-as-teachers is a popular teaching model in many professional degree programs, wherein each student selects a topic from a preapproved list of options, researches the topic, and then shares their knowledge with the rest of the class. This assignment gives students the opportunity to hone their teaching skills while also pushing them to investigate course topics on a deeper level. For this assignment, each student will select a topic related to Virtual Private Networks (VPNs) or Secure Web Browsers (Firefox, Brave). They will then record a 15–20 minute presentation on the topic they have selected.

Midterm Assignment (40 points):

Review web data privacy statements of library/information organizations.

Develop a privacy policy for a fictional information organization of your choice.

Policy should include: 1) What data is collected about users, 2) how is the data used, 3) who has access to the data, 4) how long may the data be retained, 5) who is responsible for reviewing the policy, and 6) what is the procedure if a user wishes to challenge the policy?

Final Project (60 points):

Students have two options for the final project: 1) A privacy integration plan, or 2) a privacy lesson plan. Both options will require a final submission of either: A) A recorded (20–30 minute) presentation, or B) a written (~1500 words) report.

Throughout the semester, you should make notes about how you would apply your new knowledge of online information privacy to informing services within an organization (library, business, nonprofit) of your choice. In this final project, you are asked to articulate and justify a plan either for integrating better privacy practices into their selected organization or offering instruction to users/patrons on safe privacy practices.

What Does This Class Accomplish?

This class is designed to not solely focus on the anonymous web, but rather introduce students to a wide array of information access and privacy topics, which includes the anonymous web. This includes topics like filter bubbles (discussed in Chapter 2) and VPNs. Additionally, it introduces students to a range of historically important scholarly contributions, including Leiner et al.'s History of the Internet and Goldschlag, Reed, and Syverson's early work with the onion routing technology that became the Tor network. Assignments offer variety, focusing on different aspects of web privacy, using learning principles like Universal Design for Learning. These elements, of course, are just suggestions – not necessarily objectively the best way of organizing things.

Teaching Methods

Use of Analogy

Earlier in this book, we employed a nesting box analogy for how the Tor network works. Here, we return to that analogy, to explore how it, and similar analogies, can be used to teach about all facets of the anonymous web. Several recent publications across a variety of disciplines have championed the use of analogies as a pedagogical device for improving student learning and retention of complex subject matter (Gogolla and Stevens, 2018; Houle, 2018; Kurt, 2019). Use of analogy in teaching is an example of positive transfer, where past learning helps a learner assimilate or contextualize new learning (Sousa, 2017, p. 155). While a highly technical topic – like how information systems operate – may be inaccessible to a learner without educational background in this area, an analogy that employs concepts – like two people having a conversation – can help the learner understand the underlying mechanism/principles behind the information system's operation. While they may not understand what a "router" is, they will understand what a mail carrier is.

The challenge for an instructor is to develop an analogy that is both meaningful for the student and is accurate enough that helps that student learn (in a basic sense) about the true nature of the topic. The analogy cannot be so forced that it provides no true clarity. Students must be able to see clear connections in the content and it must be such that it draws their attention (Houle, 2018). In the following sections, we discuss how analogy was utilized to help teach about how the Tor network/anonymous web operates and outcomes of instructional sessions that did and did not employ the analogy.

The Nesting Box Analogy

Imagine you have a message you wish to convey to a friend who lives across town. You are unable to leave your home, so you will need some help to have the message delivered. The message is also of a private nature, so you do not want anyone but your friend to be able to read it.

Thankfully, your town offers a volunteer network of people who have agreed to carry messages for anyone with privacy. All you need to do is write your message down, and put it in a box. Once your note is in the box, you put a lock on it with a code that is only known by your friend. You know that your neighbor is on the privacy network, so you put your locked box inside another, slightly larger box. This box is locked as well, with a code that is only known by your neighbor. Next, you just give your box to your neighbor. Once he gets it, he uses his code to open the outside box and takes out the inner box with your personal note. Since he does not know your code, he is not able to open the inner box and read the message. He just knows that he is not the person who the inner box is intended for, so he puts it in another box and locks it with the code for the next person on the volunteer network. That person gets the box, opens the outer box, realizes it is not for them and puts it in another box with a code only known by the next person on the volunteer network. Eventually, your friend will receive the box and open it. Your friend will know the code for the inner box so they will be able to open it and read it.

Using this method your personal note for your friend is private and protected from your house to your friend. Even if someone were able to intercept the box between members of the volunteer network, they would not be able to open the boxes without the codes. Even the members of the volunteer network are only able to open the box with their code, they cannot open the final message. Also, if someone were to intercept the boxes, they would not know where it came from. They interceptor would not know who the message came from. This adds additional privacy for you, no one would be aware that you were talking with your friend.

Relating the Actual Operation of Tor to the Analogy

The actual Tor network is a bit more complicated that this simplified nesting box analogy. When a computer connects to the Tor network and sends a message out, it is actually placed in multiple layers of encryption. Think of this like an onion – with layers of encryption. This is how the Tor network actually got its name. It originally stood for The Onion Router.

Teaching Ideas

Using the analogy would be useful to explain how the Tor network operates, how it provides routing, privacy, and security.

Router/Users

When someone joins the volunteer network, this is similar to the way the Tor network creates nodes on the network. As each device is added to the network, it registers itself with the Tor.

Routing

At each router on the network, a layer of encryption is removed and more are added before it is passed to the next router on the network.

Understanding Privacy

Since the primary goal of the Tor network is privacy using the analogy is useful to understanding how privacy is achieved. Since only the starting and ending users can open the message, there is privacy in the message. Since each router along the way can only remove part of the layers of encryption, the private message is secure. Anyone who intercepts the message would not be able to read the message due to the layers of encryption added.

On Network/Off Network

The idea of passing messages around inside the network should provide understanding of the security and privacy that is offered. For any message that is intended for a recipient on the Tor network (.onion site), the privacy and security is present. The analogy could be extended to the idea of recipients off the network. The idea of security when the message is decrypted and carried off the network could be explained. This could lead to the discussion of HTTPS connections.

Tracking/Logging

Since each router on the Tor network does not keep a log of messages passing through them, extra layers of security are added. Also, the idea of tracking messages as they move around is very difficult since the routing techniques used provide extra protection.

Some routers on the network can add markers or some other kinds of identifiers to the boxes as they move around. This would allow them to sort of 'track' the boxes as they move. This starts to break the privacy and security of the network since someone could potentially see where boxes came from and where they are going.

Weaknesses

It should be obvious to students that the passing of messages from user to user will take more time than to just pass the message to the friend. Privacy and security take extra time.

The idea of bad routers (or neighbors) could be introduced. It is possible that a bad neighbor could keep track of all the boxes passing through their house. They could make copies of the boxes as they get them. Eventually it might be possible to use an exploit against the locks on the boxes and open them.

Testing the Analogy in Teaching

To test the analogy, it was used in an online conference session for professional librarians, who have a postgraduate education but generally (with exceptions) have a limited knowledge of systems and cybersecurity. We contend that this is an important population to provide this education, considering that libraries provide public Internet access to a wide swath of the population, including many who have limited computer literacy. This population is also likely on-par with the average undergraduate systems student in terms of their technical knowledge.

The analogy was utilized during an online conference session in May 2020, with attendees asked to evaluate the efficacy of it. Reception, as shown in Figure 6.1, was overwhelming positive: 22 of 28 attendees suggested that they were able to comprehend how Tor works after this session, while feedback at other conference presentations suggested that very few – less than 1/2 – felt comfortable that they understood how the network worked after a

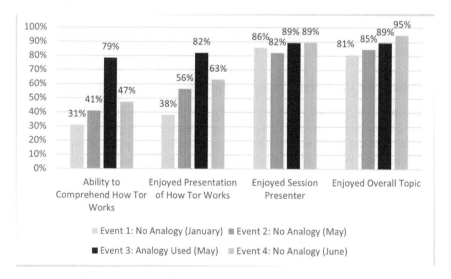

Figure 6.1 Learner Feedback Following Presentations With and Without Analogy

presentation that did not utilize analogy. Two perceptions – whether learners enjoyed the session presenter(s) and enjoyed the overall topic – remained relatively stable and positive.

Analogy proved useful in instructing a nontechnical audience on the details of how the Tor network works. This finding is important for emphasizing the importance for this platform (and similar platforms) and demystifying systems topics. As many library students and librarians have interest in technical topics relevant to their occupation but may not have sufficient background training to understand systems principles, this analogy solution may make these topics more accessible. These efforts may be expanded upon to include the use of analogy for other technical topics.

Anonymous Web as a Focus of System Analysis and Design

In courses where system analysis and design is a topic (maybe not information literacy courses, but certainly some courses at library and information science schools), the anonymous web can be used an example of the systems analysis and design process. Goldschlag, Syverson, and Reed's articles published in 1996, 1997, 1998, and 1999 that describe the development of the Tor network on top of the existing Internet infrastructure indicates clearly how a need was identified within the existing system (for enhanced privacy), a solution was developed and then refined over time, and implemented and evolved based on user testing. Onion routing can be both a relevant example and an introduction to what the technology is, such that some of the mysticism surrounding the platform can be ameliorated. The schematics of how anonymous web platforms like Tor attain anonymity through their routing and encryption are useful for introducing basic concepts of networking. Chapter 2 of this book could be used as a reading for such a course module (we are cool with you sharing a copy you downloaded from the dark web, but our publisher and their attorneys may disagree).

Emphasis on Recurring Themes in Information Privacy Topics

Tomain (2020) provides ten key themes that he incorporates in his privacy courses. While the topic of these courses is information privacy *law*, we can take a look and imagine how these themes could be applied in more practical situations. We would argue that at least the first eight themes are directly relevant to our mission with this book.

Tomain's (2020) themes:

1 Surveillance: Focusing on how user behavior is tracked online. Tomain recommends Zuboff's 2019 book "The Age of Surveillance Capitalism" as a primer on this topic. "Surveillance capitalism" is seen as the current state of economic systems in which personal data has become commodified (in ways that we discuss throughout this book).

2 Aggregation: Data aggregation is the process through which data is collected together – often from several different databases – in order to create summaries about individuals or groups.

3 Distinction between "public" and "private" data: There is a difference between using data provides by the Institute for Museum and Library Services' Public Library Survey and that collected from users on a library's website.

4 Power: The size of a social media network like Facebook or Twitter alone is enough to raise concern about the power they have over our data, regardless of the policies they have in-place to protect it.

5 Human dignity: People have the right to their own thoughts, deeds, and communication without public scrutiny.

6 Autonomy and consent: People have a right to decide what information is shared with others.

7 Obscurity: "The right to be forgotten."

8 Purposes of privacy: Privacy can further both individual and collective ends. Tomain uses the example of the use of the pseudonym "Publius" in the Federalist papers.

9 Proper legal classification of privacy – perhaps not particularly relevant to our discussion here.

10 Courts versus Legislatures versus Administrators – ditto.

In the context of anonymous web education, these themes point to a justification for the use of the networks. They set the scene like the first module in a semester-long course or the first 20 minutes of a lecture. You can imagine organizing course topics around these ten themes (even if perhaps not in name), in a course on data and privacy.

Integrating Information Privacy Into Information Literacy Instruction

Information literacy sessions are often over-condensed as it is, so suggesting that we incorporate yet another topic may seem insane. However, the purpose of this section is to do just that. Why? First, because it is a topic of utmost importance to students that commonly gets overlooked in university orientations and first-year courses. Second, it focuses directly on information, albeit strategies on how to preserve it rather than to seek or use it. Information privacy dovetails nicely into the topics already the focus of instructional libraries: misinformation and access.

While the anonymous web may be a part of this instruction (and, indeed, that will be the focus of most of the rest of this section), it is not necessary in order to convey an effective message (though it may be a useful attention grabber, imagine a course entitled, "Fake news, the dark web, and data literacy: Your Internet toolkit"). Selecting secure passwords, carefully choosing a web browser, and monitoring security settings are all helpful privacy tactics that can be readily incorporated into information literacy instruction with broaching on the anonymous web. They will provide invaluable tools for defending oneself from modern attacks. They can also be fairly easily reduced to a set of talking or bullet points that can be sprinkled among other discussion (like selecting the right browser/search engine that balances privacy and ease of use for finding reliable information). This way of teaching normalizes privacy as one aspect to consider in ones' work, rather than focus a whole session on the topic and risk losing students who become "bored."

We are not the first to suggest integrating privacy into information literacy instruction. In a 2011 study, Magnuson argues that online privacy, or "reputation management," is directly related to information literacy standards through the inclusion of "ethics of information." This gives a direct mandate for libraries to engage in privacy instruction as part of information literacy work. Magnuson provides five ways in which librarians can use their position to promote privacy practices:

- Expanding the ethics conversation to include discussion of how sharing private information can increase risk of that information being accessed by others.
- Promote user empowerment on social media, focusing on what information they can safely share rather than that which poses risks.
- Set an example by making the library's own privacy policy widely available.
- Make connections between the work and activities in which students are interested and the need to preserve privacy.
- Celebrate privacy through events like Privacy Awareness week (in May of each year).

Wissinger (2017) discusses the need to move the concept of "privacy literacy" from theory to practice. In introducing the topic of privacy literacy, Wissinger provides two different definitions of privacy literacy, which are:

1 "[privacy literacy is] the understanding that consumers have of the information landscape with which they interact and their responsibilities with that landscape" (Langenderfer and Miyazaki, 2009, p. 383). This is obviously a very broad definition that is really more descriptive of information ethics in general than information privacy specifically.
2 "One's level of understanding and awareness of how much information is tracked and used in online environments and how that information can retain or lose its private nature" (Givens, 2014, p. 531). This definition is much more specific and useful for our purposes.

Additionally, Wissinger discusses Rotman's (2009) framework for privacy literacy, which consists of five elements:

- Understanding how personal information is used online.
- Recognizing the various places personal information may be shared online.
- Realizing the consequences of sharing personal information online.
- Evaluating the risks and benefits of sharing personal information online.
- Deciding when to share personal information online.

This framework aligns with Givens (2014) definition but provides an even more specific list of items that are all actionable (e.g., you can improve your ability to make informed decisions about when to share personal information online).

Wissinger notes that, though there is not privacy literacy instruction offered by most libraries, the ACRL standards clearly support the inclusion of privacy concepts in information literacy instruction. Privacy literacy initiatives are readily supported by library associations and grant funding organizations like the Institute of Museum and Library Services. Wissinger makes note of a $35,000 grant project at San Jose Public Library, and a privacy bibliography developed and offered by Pennsylvania State University.

Bawden and Robinson (2020) suggest a privacy literacy framework that may be integrated into information literacy skills work. In this framework, the authors apply Luciano Floridi's theorizing in the area of information privacy to the concept of privacy literacy. The proposed Floridian approach includes six elements or understandings of privacy concepts:

- Understanding of the nature of privacy itself (what does "having privacy" actually mean?)
- An overarching philosophical and ethical system (justification of how privacy is understood based on empirical observation – universal knowledge of these values)
- An ontology of information that defines aspects of the information environment relevant to the nature of privacy
- Types of privacy – understanding that there are many forms of privacy of which informational privacy is one; Bawden and Robinson cite Koops et al. (2017), who list nine types of privacy: Bodily, intellectual, spatial, decisional, communicational, associational, proprietary, behavioral, and informational
- The influence of digital technologies, considering they can both be used to defend privacy/anonymity (e.g., the Anonymous web) or be used to breech it (e.g., social media)
- Information frictions, "all forces opposing free flow of information and data, and to the amount of work needed to access and process information" (Bawden and Robinson, 2020, p. 1034)

Bawden and Robinson conceive privacy literacy as a metaliteracy (along with digital literacy, data literacy, information literacy, and many others). Applying the six elements of the Floridian model above to the concept of privacy literacy, there are several points to be considered, which could be adapted when considering information literacy instruction. Information privacy should be considered in both online and offline contexts (or what is called, in Floridian terms, "onlife"). There is a blurring of the lines between the two. Privacy literacy involves understanding how personal information is used onlife, how it can be shared and where friction exists, the consequences of sharing personal information including both risks and benefits, and making personal decisions that reflect balancing informational frictions.

A One-Off IL Session with Integration of Privacy Literacy Concepts

In this scenario, we will imagine an information literacy instructional session at an academic library. Start the privacy literacy section of the instruction by asking, "what tools does the university offer or are freely available to you?" Begin by mentioning anything the university owns a license for, such as a VPN. Show where to find these tools and succinctly describe how they work. During this time, you would be walking the class through the steps on your computer, illustrating both auditorily and visually what needs to be done. For instance,

> "Through the Department of Information Technology's website, our university has access to SmartVPN. A VPN, or virtual private network, is a type of network tunnel that securely connects a user to a website, preventing potential surveillance or data theft from third parties. To find it, navigate to the Information Technology website, click on the 'downloads' tab, and under the list of resources on the downloads page, select the SmartVPN option. In order to download, you will need to enter your university username and password. The download will then initiate and you will follow the instructions on the screen just as with any computer download."

This demonstration should be very similar to how an instructional librarian would typically provide instruction on accessing the library's databases or downloading and using Zotero. It need not be a detailed history on what a VPN is, even if you think providing detailed information would be best. Making students into experts is not the purpose of a one-off instructional session, especially when there are so many other information literacy topics on which to also touch. Here, you might, however, mention a few of the concepts associated with overall privacy literacy, in order to stress the importance of a VPN. This example touches on several of Rotman's (2009) concepts:

"We should all be aware that we are constantly producing data – data that can reveal important insights about who we are as consumers. This data is highly valuable and companies and attackers will twist all sorts of boundaries – imagined and real – in order to get it. One example is cookies. Not the kind that you eat, but the kind that contains data about your browsing behavior that follows you from site to site as you peruse the web. This data should not be something which you want to readily give away, even if you are not engaging in any suspect behavior. Fortunately, there are tool that are designed to help preserve your privacy. A VPN is one of them, secure browsers like Brave is another. If you really want to ensure the highest level of anonymity on the web you might consider a browser like Tor..."

When speaking about Tor with college students, it may be advisable to skip the history lesson and focus on the anonymity. We do not encourage hiding what the anonymous web is, but omission, especially in a one-off session, is permissible. We would advise mentioning that Tor is a specialized network that uses principles of encryption and specialized routing to protect users from surveillance and censorship. Then, just as showing how to access the VPN, provide a demonstration of where and how to download Tor. As with anything that you teach, take time for questions and be willing to admit when you do not know an answer (it is okay – as this book has shown, this is a broad and complex topic!).

Given all the considerations outlined in this chapter, you might ask, "would it not be better for some IT person to offer this training instead of me?" I do not know that it would necessarily be better, but it might lighten the instructional librarian's already overbearing load. So, yes, if your university has the resources and willing IT personnel to teach about these technologies, that is great. But it is likely that they will not and, if they do, it will be some boring online module that we all know you just click through to the end and guess on the three questions so you can be done with it. IT people are not teachers. Many have no interest in teaching, or really interacting with students in a non-"where's the problem?" way. Librarians are teachers, whether they thought that was what they were going to be when the enrolled in library school or not, that is where they all end up. So why do everything possible to employ their teaching expertise into claiming another domain (student privacy literacy) that demonstrates value to their parent entity (university, government, business)?

This chapter introduces some approaches to integrating instruction about the anonymous web and related privacy technologies into information literacy instruction and provides a framework for a course on this topic. Each lesson must ultimately be tailored to the unique speaker/situation/audience to which it will be presented, so the concepts in this chapter are meant only as ideas that can be combined and altered to develop the most effective sessions for your needs.

References

Bawden, D. and Robinson, L. (2020), "'The dearest of our possessions': Applying Floridi's information privacy concept in models of information behavior and information literacy", *Journal of the Association for Information Science and Technology*, Vol. 71, No. 9. https://doi.org/10.1002/asi.24367

Belshaw, S. H., Nodeland, B., Underwood, L., and Colaiuta, A. (2019), "Teaching about the dark web in criminal justice programs at the community college and university levels", *Journal of Cybersecurity Education, Research and Practice*, Vol. 2019, No. 2, Article 5.

Givens, Cherie L. (2014), *Information privacy fundamentals for librarians and information professionals*, Rowman & Littlefield, Lanham, MD.

Gogolla, M. and Stevens, P. (2018), "Teaching modeling in computer science as an ecosystem: A provocative analogy", *Computer Science Education*, Vol. 28, No. 1, pp. 5–22.

Houle, S. (2018), "Talk shows and t-tests: Applying an analogy from late-night television to biostatistics in an introductory drug information course", *Currents in Pharmacy Teaching and Learning*, Vol. 10, No. 11, pp. 1474–1477.

Koops, Bert-Jaap, Newell, Bryce Clayton, Timan, Tjerk, Škorvánek, Ivan, Chokrevski, Tomislav and Galič, Maša. (2017), "A typology of privacy", *University of Pennsylvania Journal of International Law*, Vol. 38, No. 2, p. 483.

Kurt, S. (2019), "An analogy activity for teaching chemical reaction and collision theory from perspectives of pre-service science teachers", *International Journal of Environmental and Science Education*, Vol. 14, No. 9, pp. 521–534.

Langenderfer, J. and Miyazaki, A. D. (2009), "Privacy in the information economy", *Journal of Consumer Affairs*, Vol. 43, No. 3, pp. 380–388.

Magnuson, L. (2011), "Promoting privacy: Online and reputation management as an information literacy skill", *College & Research Libraries News*, Vol. 72, No. 3, pp. 137–140.

Rotman, D. (2009), "*Are you looking at me?: Social media and privacy literacy*", iConference 2009. http://hdl.handle.net/2142/15339

Sousa, D. A. (2017), *How the brain learns*, Sage Publishing, Thousand Oaks, CA.

Tomain, Joseph A. (2020), "Teaching information privacy law", *Washburn Law Journal*, Vol. 59, pp. 445.

Wissinger, C. L. (2017), "Privacy literacy: From theory to practice", *Communications in Information Literacy*, Vol. 11, No. 2, pp. 378–389.

7 A Role for Library and Information Science Researchers in Anonymous Web Research

Most of the anonymous web platforms have their own research program that focuses on understanding who uses the platform and how the platform can be made to run more efficiently and securely. Additionally, many researchers in the areas of computer science and systems research the operation of the network itself, hypothesizing potential attacks that could be successful against the network and solutions that can patch vulnerabilities before they are seized upon by bad actors. These particular topics may not be of interest to social science researchers, but there are many ways to examine elements of the anonymous web from a social science perspective as well, by looking at how users communicate and look for and share information with one another. These elements of the anonymous web have not yet been explored in much detail. There is ample opportunity for a new generation of researchers to pick up a research specialization in these areas.

Library and information science (LIS) researchers can play a major role in advancing anonymous web research, given their focus on information behavior and management. This chapter discusses some ways in which LIS researchers are already exploring different aspects of the anonymous web and proposes additional topics that may be compelling for future researchers. It also discusses some of the research methods that may be utilized to explore these topics and potential hazards and pitfalls to be aware of when researching the anonymous web.

Anonymous Web Research Topics

Natural Language Processing

Language processing algorithms can be used to parse content uploaded on the anonymous web. This process could help to monitor and enforce some sort of appropriate use policy, without necessarily compromising privacy and security of users. This extends to nonlanguage content, like photos and images, where several groups of researchers have developed classification algorithms to identify inappropriate content (Fidalgo et al., 2019). Developing and incorporating this type of technology into the monitoring

DOI: 10.4324/9781003093732-8

of anonymous websites, while it would undeniably face some pushback by traditional users of the network, may help create a more welcoming anonymous web experience for the general user.

Authorship Attribution

How do you form a consensus on who authored certain content when the platform they used is designed to promote anonymity? By using similar technology to the natural language processing above to match linguistic qualities in the writing. Each person has their own unique writing style – different terms and punctuation they use, different ways of phrasing things – and this fact can clue us in to the author of an anonymous work. This process is used in the digital humanities to help determine authorship of books where no author is known, or to confirm whether a work attributed to a certain author likely was or was not actually authored by that individual (e.g., Shakespeare).

What is the value of such an authorship attribution tool on the anonymous web? There are at least two that we can imagine. First, in the case that the author used a pseudonym to publish something, this tool could be used to confirm, based on the author's prior content, that the new content was actually produced by the same author rather than a different person using the same pseudonym. Second, in the case that the content shared is something illegal, and was posted anonymously, it may be possible to identify the author through linguistic analysis, particularly if the author has produced many other writings for comparison. This is like what detectives in those crime shows do when they bring in a linguistic expert to examine letters left by a murderer. So, this tool could be useful both for policing and settling disputes on a platform that is otherwise anonymous.

Extending and Incorporating the Tor Network in New Platforms

Suppose you like the capabilities of anonymous web platforms like Tor but think "I can do better." There are several emerging networks that employ the Tor protocol (using onion routing) as part of a new service that promises even more privacy, security, or user-friendly interface. Though research on how to develop one of these platforms may be too advanced, from a systems and programming perspective, for the average librarian to participate in, some information scientists may be interested in undertaking such a project, and the user-centered philosophy extolled in LIS education may be useful in developing a system that best meets the preferences and needs of users. This development of utilizing Tor as a backbone for further innovation has emerged in works like Diaz et al. (2021), with their proposed BChain platform, and Hiller et al. (2019), who proposed onion routing as a way to secure communications on an Internet of Things.

Adoption of Tor and User Information Behavior

Who is using Tor? Why? How? Who should be using it and what barriers stand in their way? These are fundamental questions that librarians are situated to explore. Researchers like Harbouth and Pape (2019) have examined what personal and environmental factors contribute to the adoption of privacy-enhancing platforms like Tor, finding that concerns about privacy being compromised and a lack of trust predict user behavior in the adoption of these platforms. Lindner and Xiao (2020) similarly examined reasons for using Tor, documenting the drive to avoid surveillance while using the web. Further research may document who is adopting Tor at the greatest rates and possibly look at political and other affiliations as a clue.

A few recent studies of information behavior on the anonymous web have also been conducted. Hu et al. (2020) classified behaviors of group of anonymous web users based on an analysis of traffic on the platforms (most of the platforms discussed in this book share traffic statistics freely online) Perhaps most notably, Haasio, Harviainen, and Savolainen (2020) explored the information needs of drug users who utilize the dark web marketplaces. By understanding some of the rationale behind why people use anonymous web platforms to engage in illegal activities – and how they accomplish it – it may be possible to develop better interventions to prevent the spread of this activity. To what extent does censorship of discussion involving drug use drive the user deeper into the depths of the dark web while not deterring the actual problematic behavior? This is an important question to answer if we want to know about the effectiveness of current policy and intervention.

Lastly, it is beneficial to better understand how have and how can organizations support the safe adoption and use of Tor. In a 2021 paper, Lund and Beckstrom ("we") examined library mission statements and policy, looking for alignment between these policies/values and those of the anonymous web (Lund and Beckstrom, 2021). We concluded that our findings indicate two things: 1) That the anonymous web would help further the mission of libraries by preserving the privacy and security of patrons, and 2) that some small yet significant changes would need to be made to library policy to support the adoption of the anonymous web, most importantly that there be separate computer use policies applicable to computers used by children and those used by adults. Some detailed case studies of libraries actually providing access to the anonymous web and reflecting these changes in their policies and user education would possibly be helpful for other libraries to follow suit.

Constructive Community Interaction

Since the beginning of information behavior theory in LIS, there has been interest in how communities form and collectively behave. This includes what Elfreda Chatman, in her small world's theory, calls "social norms," "social roles," and "normative behaviors." On the anonymous web, a number of organically forming communities have emerged. Yes, this includes groups that discuss and/or share illicit content, which will undoubtedly receive the greatest public interest, but also communities centered on shared political or religious beliefs, or personal experiences. There are communities for transgender students, political dissidents under oppressive regimes, and religious minorities in countries like North Korea. These communities all have at least some characteristics that align remarkably well with Chatman's small worlds.

By better understanding these communities that have formed on the anonymous web, it may be possible to foster an environment that provides a safe space for important discussions. The people participating in these discussions may be those who would not otherwise have or seek any outlet for connecting with those in a similar situation (i.e., they may be resistant to the idea of participating in a social or counseling group). This makes them a vulnerable population to study, but also one that would provide great value to better understand. Researchers may be able to embed themselves in these communities and deeply explore what can be done to support these important discussions. Conversely, if the community is one that perpetuates illegal or harmful behavior, better understanding of the group's workings may help develop interventions to mitigate the role and influence of these groups. Because this type of research would likely require direct interaction between the researcher and members of these groups, it would require ethical board approval and adherence to appropriate ethical standards (i.e., informed consent of participants being studied).

Anonymous Web and COVID-19

The COVID-19 pandemic has presented new reasons why people might utilize the anonymous web: To find reliable information in countries where misleading, dangerous information has ruled (or indulge in conspiracy theories though reliable information IS available), to communicate about treatments and strategy. However, the most compelling reason that users have adopted the anonymous web during this time has been to access drug markets. By "drug markets" we do not mean illicit drug markets, per say, but instead those that offer drugs that have been hypothesized to help treat COVID-19 itself, like Hydroxychloroquine. During the peak of the pandemic in nations like India, these drugs became highly valued and extremely scarce, leading to a black market. Vaccines developed a similar market once they had emerged (Bracci et al., 2021a; 2021b).

The impact of an emergency situation on the use of the anonymous web should serve as a learning opportunity for future experiences. Already, library researchers have documented the process of updating library websites and policy during the pandemic, providing new services, and understanding changes in user behavior (Walsh and Rana, 2020; Anderson, Fisher, and Walker, 2021; Wang and Lund, 2020). Similar documentation should be made for use of privacy-preserving platforms during this pandemic situation and this will be more challenging as the pandemic progresses further into our rearview mirror.

Methods for Anonymous Web Research

Analysis of Traffic Data

Usage data for the three major anonymous web platforms discussed in this book (Tor, I2P, and Freenet) is provided by the sites, either as a page on the platform's download site or as a separate website (or eepsite) within the platform. The Tor project's research data page (as of Summer 2021) is located at https://community.torproject.org/user-research/. This page includes all reports Tor has published based on its own research, but also includes a data hub for usage data so that researchers can perform their own analyses.

What value does an analysis of traffic data provide? For one thing, it can illustrate relationships between major events and usage of the anonymous web. For instance, when a country bans a certain social media site, the use of Tor may show a bounce. When China and Iran tried to block use of the Tor network, the use of bridges – which, you may recall, are hidden relays designed to circumvent censorship attempts – experienced a sizeable growth in those countries. The fact that eight of the ten countries with the greatest usage of Tor are countries known for regular censorship of the web likely indicates what type of people use these platforms (namely, those seeking to circumvent censorship attempts). People simply trust numbers above all else, and analysis of traffic data provides hard numbers around which to construct an argument.

Content Analysis

Content analysis is likely the most common method used in research involving the anonymous web (Takaaki and Atsuo, 2019). The "content" to analyze is easy enough to collect from the various forums and websites within the anonymous web. The analysis may be guided by some sort of a priori framework or set of hypotheses to be evaluated based on the text; otherwise, the analysis may be exploratory, where themes are identified by reading through the content before progressing to further analysis of the content. The purpose of content analysis within this context of the anonymous web is to analyze language use and communication, hoping to reveal some deeper meaning.

Content analysis has become a popular method because, assuming the content is shared on a public forum, there is likely no need for an ethics review, and there is no need to conduct lengthy data collection like with interviews or a questionnaire. The text can simply be downloaded to a platform like Excel, Word, or NVIVO (qualitative analysis software) and analyzed. This, for instance, was what was done in Haasio, Harviainen, and Savolainen's (2020) study. They analyzed 9300 messages on a popular dark web forum for drug users, using a theoretical framework that was heavily influenced by Elfreda Chatman's information poverty and small worlds concepts.

Text Mining

Text and data mining methods have become of increasing interest in recent years in LIS research (Ma and Lund, 2021). The anonymous web provides a broad collection of texts for analysis that can reveal insight about the people that use these platforms. Text mining is similar, in many ways, to content analysis, but utilizes automated processes to identify themes in a text as opposed to manual classification. There are many types of text mining, ranging from a simple word frequency count (which can be managed by Microsoft Word or Excel just as easy as any other platform) to sentiment analysis, clustering, linguistic pattern recognition, which would require a programming language like Python or a data mining software like RapidMiner in order to perform the analysis.

For those interested in how to conduct text and data mining on the anonymous web, there are many excellent resources that cover the topic in greater detail than we do here. Spitters, Verbruggen, and van Staalduinen (2014), as well as Wang and Goldberg (2013), provide a classification of dark websites based on the results of a text analysis – detailing the process they used to accomplish this goal – for example. Silge and Robinson's (2017) book *Text Mining with R: A Tidy Approach* is recommended for those interested in learning more about text mining approaches.

Ethnography

In an ethnographic study, on aims to immerse themselves in a culture, in order to better understand the motivations behind beliefs and practices, or otherwise describe the culture as it is experienced by an individual who is actually a member of that culture. Ethnographic studies employ a variety of data collection methods, from observation to interviews to textual analysis.

An example of an ethnographic-type study in the context of the anonymous web is one that one of this book's authors performed in early 2021 to explore cryptocurrency pump-and-dump forums. The idea behind a cryptocurrency pump-and-dump, in short, is as follows:

1 A group of individuals will first work together to select a specific cryptocurrency (generally, one that seems undervalued) and purchase it in large quantities.
2 Members of this group then promote this cryptocurrency on social media, with overinflated claims (i.e., lies) about its potential for massive short-term growth.

3 The members of the group "sell high" while the price is skyrocketing due to the buying frenzy sparked by the social media buzz.
4 When those tricked by the scam realize what is going on, they sell off the cryptocurrency, causing the price to crater back down to where it was initially.

Cryptocurrency pump-and-dumps reside in a legal gray area. Most forms of pump-and-dump schemes are illegal, but cryptocurrency pump-and-dumps are not policed (likely due to the fact that they are relatively new) though they would likely still be considered illegal and could be policed at any time. Unsurprisingly, the pump-and-dump groups are not visible in public forums, but rather exist on hidden chat forums, on sites like Discord – or on forums on the anonymous web. With my interest in cryptocurrencies, I (Brady) managed to come across one of these forums on the anonymous web. The groups are selective (they do not want to have too many members, because that would defeat the purpose of the pump-and-dump) but are generally welcoming when they are looking for new members (like when a group has just started up). This gave me a point of entry into one of the newer groups, where I was able to interact with fellow members and understand their motivations for being a member.

Membership in a cryptocurrency pump-and-dump group was not solely motivated by monetary drives, but also social and political ones. The best way to describe the members of the group might be "anarcho-capitalist," but they felt they had been economically wronged by the government, by big businesses, and by consumer culture and had a sense of collectivism within their own group where it was not like a Mad Max free-for-all situation. There was a lot of ranting about how the pump-and-dump schemes were righteous, because so many had stolen from them. I do not believe that was a real justification, more of an excuse to feed their own ethically corrupt behavior; after all, with their schemes, they were not stealing from those businesses and governments, they were stealing from the common man, often broke young adults. But the mythology was important to the cohesion of the group.

These types of observations are those that can be made using an ethnographic approach. Through observing the discussions among members of the group, and engaging them in discussion yourself, it is possible to reveal how the world they created is sustained and why. Ostensibly, the actual reason it was created and sustained was to make money, but the myth they told themselves is what allowed them to participate in what otherwise was clearly unethical behavior. So how do you effectively police these groups? Do you try to break them up – in that case the myth is still sustained – or do you go after the myth itself? This is a question that can be asked only because we understand the group from the perspective of the myth, rather than the greed that is apparent from the surface. Other studies can employ similar approaches to examine other communities on the anonymous web and better understand the true motivations behind sustaining such a community on the platform.

Potential Hazards and Other Considerations

Researchers of the anonymous web should note that most people using the platform could be considered to be a part of some sensitive population, and that they are using the platform specifically to preserve their anonymity, so extra care (even beyond normal) must be taken to ensure the sanctity of the study and its data. Anyone seeking to conduct an interview or ethnographic study, where data about specific individuals will be collected, should be well of best practices for conducting such studies with a vulnerable population. LeCompte and Schensul's (2010) book *Designing and Conducting Ethnographic Research* is recommended as a primer on conducting this type of study and considering ethical risks.

Another risk for anonymous web researchers is allowing your priors/beliefs about the anonymous to influence your analysis and cause you to draw false conclusions. It is evident from the titles of research articles pertaining to the anonymous web that many are drawn to the criminal elements on the platform. As this book has intended to illuminate, there is much more to the anonymous web than just criminal actions. Even more than that, though, is that it is problematic to enter studying a group with the prior that you believe everyone you will study is some amoral criminal. Generally, everyone (even criminals) has a perfectly rational justification, at some level, for doing what they do. It should be the purpose of research to examine these justifications, not to treat the subjects of inquiry as those they are not human. The anonymous web should be portrayed as a context for the study, much like a "nursing home," "school," or "Facebook," not as something that is inherently good or bad or from which you can make inferences about the user simply because they use it.

Similarly, the best studies of the anonymous web are those that avoid chasing the sensational. Does including keywords like "dark web," "drugs," and "crime" boost your views? Probably so. Is that what you really intend to study, though? Unless you are a criminology researcher, probably not. As mentioned above, the anonymous web probably serves only as a context for your study and the aim of your study is not to investigate crime but to understand human beliefs and motivations. So even if the subjects of your study are, by definition, criminals, think about whether that is the element of their character that you are actually examining. Furthermore, studies of criminal elements on the anonymous web are so… passe. Why not study groups that deserve greater attention and for whom your study may actually have a profound impact? Groups like those for political, social, and sexual minorities? Those for intellectuals? We are inclined to fixate on crime like we are 20th century yellow journalists. But we should not desire to be Charles Foster Kane, but rather a great intellectual who serves as a neutral observer and acknowledges the many benefits as well as the risks of the anonymous web.

Bibliometric Studies

Another opportunity for anonymous web research is through bibliometric studies. Bibliometric studies analyze the bibliographic data for a set of publications on a particular topic. The objective of this analysis is to identify important authors, publication venues, and topic themes, with this information being used to inform future research by suggesting new topics and best places to publish research. An example of some of the elements that may be included in a bibliometric analysis is discussed below.

Example with Tor Studies

This study is based on publications relating to the Tor browser (identified using the search terms "Tor," "Onion Routing," "Onion Router," "Tor browser") between the years of 1995 and 2020. 565 relevant articles were retrieved from pertinent Ebsco databases (Library and Information Science Source and Computer Source). Author, title, keywords, and publisher/publication information was collected. Keywords for articles can be analyzed in VosViewer, a free bibliometric analysis software. A keyword co-occurrence visualization shows the most common terms used in articles about Tor and illustrates relationships among terms that are used in close conjunction with one another.

Figure 7.1 is the keyword co-occurrence visualization for the Tor studies. Keywords are grouped, essentially, into four groups: On the top-left side of the

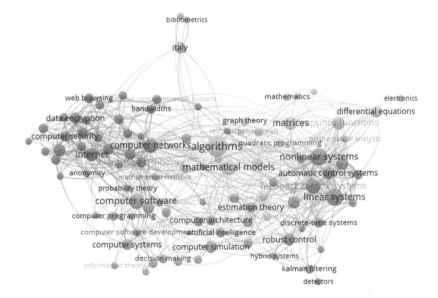

Figure 7.1 Keyword Co-occurrence Visualization for Tor Studies

visualization are terms related to networking and encryption; on the bottom-left are terms related to software design and development; on the bottom-right are terms associated with systems theory; and on the top-right are terms related to mathematical principles of computing. What does this visualization tell us? Most existing research on the Tor network is firmly in the "hard science"/ computer science camp. There are no "behavior" or "searching" terms, nor anything about "user experience" or "user perceptions." These are areas that should be further explored – areas of opportunity for LIS researchers.

As for publishers, journals and conference proceedings associated with the Association for Computing Machinery (ACM) or the Institute of Electrical and Electronics Engineers (IEEE) dominate the landscape, with nearly half of all articles published. The Journal of the Association for Information Science and Technology (JASIST), a LIS journal, actually has the most articles that mention Tor of any single journal; however, only two other LIS journals even have a single publication relating to Tor. Most of the publication outlets are firmly within the computer science/information systems camps. Thus, again, there is considerable room for new research that presents the LIS perspective on this platform.

Studies that employ bibliometric methods have considerable opportunity to reveal further insults like the ones here. These studies may be helpful not only to identify themes and publication venues but also define an ontology for the study of the anonymous web from a LIS perspective. Because so little research has been done on the anonymous web from a LIS perspective, there is much to investigate and expand upon.

What Next?

Anonymous web research can take a variety of forms. Like with the Internet, which has entire scholarly journals dedicated to the study of it, the anonymous web is a rich and complex ecosystem, one that is distinct from the Internet as we typically discuss it in those users of the anonymous web are generally those that are seeking an elevated level of anonymity, privacy, and/ or security. Unlike the Internet, which is "researched to death" nowadays, the anonymous is relatively unexplored as a place for information seeking and community building. This provides opportunity to readers like you to be among the first to participate in anonymous web research and build out a new area of inquiry relating to these platforms.

References

Anderson, R., Fisher, K. and Walker, J. (2021), "Library consultations and a global pandemic: An analysis of consultation difficulty during COVID-19 across multiple factors", *The Journal of Academic Librarianship*, Vol. 47, No. 1, Article 102273.

Bracci, A., Nadini, M., Aliapoulios, M., McCoy, D., Gray, I., Teytelboym, A., Gallo, A. and Baronchelli, A. (2021a), "Dark web marketplaces and COVID-19: The vaccines", Retrieved from https://arxiv.org/pdf/2102.05470.pdf

Bracci, A., Nadini, M., Aliapoulios, M., McCoy, D., Gray, I., Teytelboym, A., Gallo, A. and Baronchelli, A. (2021b), "Dark web marketplaces and COVID-19: Before the vaccine", *EPJ Data Science*, Vol. 10, Article 6.

Diaz, C., Erhunmwunse, J., Goff, C., Lashgari, J. and Nguyen, G. (2021), BChain A new decentralized peer-to-peer protocol, Retrieved from https://bchain-network. xyz/

Fidalgo, E., Alegre, E., Fernandez-Robles, L. and Gonzalez-Castro, V. (2019), "Classifying suspicious content in TOR darknet through semantic attention key-point filtering", *Digital Investigation*, Vol. 30, pp. 12–22.

Haasio, A., Harviainen, J. and Savolainen, R. (2020), "Information needs of drug users on a local dark web marketplace", *Information Processing and Management*, Vol. 57, No. 2, Article 102080.

Harbouth, D. and Pape, S. (2019), "How privacy concerns and trust and risk beliefs influence users' intentions to use privacy-enhancing technologies: The case of TOR", *Proceedings of the Hawaii International Conference on System Sciences*, Vol. 52, pp. 4851-4860.

Hiller, J., Pennekamp, J., Dahlmanns, M., Henze, M., Panchenko, A. and Wehrle, K. (2019), "Tailoring onion routing to the Internet of Things: Security and privacy in untrusted environments", *IEEE Conference*, Vol. 27, pp. 1–12.

Hu, Y., Zou, F., Li, L. and Yi, P. (2020), "Traffic classification of user behaviors in TOR, I2P, ZeroNet, Freenet", *IEEE Conference on Trust, Security and Privacy in Computing and Communications*, Vol. 19, paper 20425708.

LeCompte, M. D. and Schensul, J. (2010), *Designing and conducting ethnographic research*, Altamira Press, Lanham, MD.

Lindner, A. and Xiao, T. (2020), "Subverting surveillance or accessing the dark web? Interest in the TOR anonymity network in U.S. states, 2006–2015", *Social Currents*, Vol. 7, No. 4, pp. 352–370.

Lund, B. and Beckstrom, M. (2021), "The integration of Tor into library services: An appeal to the core mission and values of libraries", *Public Library Quarterly*, Vol. 40, No. 1, pp. 60–76.

Ma, J. and Lund, B. D. (2021), "The evolution and shift of research topics and methods in library and information science", *Journal of the Association for Information Science and Technology*. https://doi.org/10.1002/asi.24474

Silge, J. and Robinson, D. (2017), *Text mining with R: A tidy approach*, O' Reilly, Sebastol, CA.

Spitters, M., Verbruggen, S. and van Staalduinen, M. (2014), "Towards a comprehensive insight into the thematic organization of the Tor hidden services", *IEEE Join intelligence and Security Informatics Conference*, 2014, pp. 220–223.

Takaaki, S. and Atsuo, I. (2019), "Dark web content analysis and visualization", *ACM International Workshop on Security and Privacy Analytics*, 2019, pp. 53–59.

Walsh, B. and Rana, H. (2020), "Continuity of academic library services during the pandemic the university of Toronto Libraries' response", *Journal of Scholarly Publishing*, Vol. 51, No. 4, pp. 237–245.

Wang, T. and Goldberg, I. (2013), "Improved website fingerprinting on Tor", *ACM Workshop on Privacy in the Electronic Society*, Vol. 12, pp. 201–212.

Wang, T. and Lund, B. (2020), "Announcement information provided by United States' public libraries during the 2020 COVID-19 pandemic", *Public Library Quarterly*, Vol. 39, No. 4, pp. 283–294.

8 Case Examples of Anonymous Web Adoption in Information Organizations

One might alternatively title this chapter "Three Short Tales of Dark Libraries." This chapter will cover three semifictionalized cases of anonymous web adoption in library and information organizations in order to further discuss and contextualize how we would recommend that you address certain circumstances that might arise when you implement or provide access to an anonymous web network in your library. Each example begins with the case itself before discussing how we, as the authors, would handle the case, while also noting, if applicable, what the library in the case example did to address the situation. We have selected three cases that we believe to be the most likely for you to encounter: Technical challenges in providing access to the anonymous web or connecting as a Tor relay; apathy/nonuse of the anonymous web services provided; and public opposition to the anonymous web.

Case 1: I'm Not Your IT Expert!

In our first case, we find Ricardo, the branch manager at Seafront Public Library, struggling to help a patron whose computer has apparently frozen while accessing a website with Tor. Ricardo is not particularly technology-inclined and knows very little about Tor, but there is no one else around to assist the patron. He does not want to hard-reset the computer (force it to shut down and then turn it back on by hitting the power button) but the patron is being impatient, and Ricardo just wants to move on to the other patrons who are awaiting his assistance. What can he do to settle this issue as quickly as possible?

How We Would Address This Issue

The technical issues you will face with an anonymous web platform are not significantly different from those that would be faced with any other computer program or web browser. Tor is already a notoriously slow browser (privacy comes at a cost), but when it entirely "freezes up" it can be particularly infuriating. It is important to remain calm in these situations because

DOI: 10.4324/9781003093732-9

there are solutions to be found but, like with any technology issue, it is easy to overlook a simple solution if you are more focused on your anger than anything else.

Now, the first thing to check when Tor is being extraordinarily slow or frozen is your Internet connection, of course, and then your connection to Tor (assuming the screen is not entirely frozen, this can be accessed from the dropdown on the top right side of the browser page). If you can navigate to the main entry screen for Tor (the one that shows up when Tor has recently updated) then there is a link to the "Tor Browser Manual," which includes a detailed section on "troubleshooting" if Tor is not working (Tor Project, 2021). If the computer is completely frozen, the troubleshooting site may be access on another computer (there is a surface web version for use on other browsers that can be accessed from torproject.org). Solving this problem may eventually require that you reset the computer, which may result in the patron losing their progress, but there are many intermediate steps that can be taken, such as disabling certain computer programs temporarily while using Tor.

It is very uncommon for an issue with Tor to result in the entire computer freezing up – that tends to be more of a problem with the computer itself. So do not blame Tor! Issues with the browser itself, though, can be relatively common and may require a computer reset or the browser to be deleted and reinstalled if the problem persists. This is likely to be the most serious issue that you will face from the user's end with Tor and, even then, it does not require much technical knowledge beyond knowing how to use a troubleshooting guide. Really, customer service skills are the biggest key in this type of situation. People really underestimate the value of having good people skills as an IT employee – just getting people to feel that they are being heard.

Case 2: What's the Use with Nonuse?

Sam is a public services librarian at Sunnycrest library who was enthusiastic about their library providing access to the Tor network. However, since they began to provide access six months ago, Sam has rarely seen anyone using or commenting on the platform. She notes that, though usage of computers provided by the library has seen an uptick after the worst of the COVID-19 pandemic passed, use of Tor has actually dropped. She wonders what has gone wrong and what she can do to bring about greater adoption of Tor by library patrons.

How We Would Address This Issue

To this issue, we have a two-part response. Our first inclination is to say, "who cares?" The goal is to provide access to these platforms so somebody can use them if they feel the need. It is not about taking a tally of how many people use it (though we understand that libraries do like to take tallies of things). In fact, spying on patrons to see if they are using Tor kind of defeats the purpose. Remember, these platforms are designed for privacy. That is the reason we are suggesting that you provide access to them. So, it follows that if someone wants privacy they may want privacy from everyone (including YOU), not just Internet Service Providers and websites. Privacy is, after all, one of the most valued rights both before and during the Internet age and that valuation extends to all potential collection of information (Kokolakis, 2017).

There is really no reason to worry about how many people are using the anonymous web once you have it implemented. These platforms are free. There is no cost-benefit analysis to be performed on that end because there is no cost, only benefit. If one person gets a benefit out of using Tor, then it is worth it. The only real question to ask regarding this issue is whether the nonuse is out of choice or due to a lack of knowledge about the platform. Only in the latter case should any measures be taken to increase awareness among patrons.

Let us say that Sam discovered that very few patrons were familiar with Tor, even though it had been available in the library for six months. Perhaps they announced that Tor would be made available in the library but failed to inform patrons about what Tor is. In that case, what better opportunity to apply some of the techniques from the anonymous web instruction chapter? Remember that most people have never heard of Tor before. They may have heard of the dark web before, but probably not in a positive light. If they are not educated about Tor, then what benefits would they know about that would lead them to use it instead of Firefox or Google Chrome that they normally use? When introducing an anonymous web platform on library computers, it is important to advertise – think about physical banners in the library as well as virtual banners on the website: "Tor Browser: Now Available for Enhanced Online Privacy." You can also "sneak" discussion of Tor into a public educational session on personal privacy or related technology topics.

So, it is not every case where having few Tor users is a "bad" thing. Many patrons may simply believe that they do not need the enhanced privacy and, while we disagree, we can respect that decision if they just prefer a different browser. If just one person is using Tor for a legitimate purpose, then it is all worth it. However, if you truly believe that the issue is a lack of awareness about the platform, well, increase awareness! You will find plenty of tips if you turn back to Chapter 6. Consider also educating those employees that work most directly with the public about the platform, as they can be crucial in seeing that this information reaches the public. But there is no need to operate some rewards program for people to use Tor or anything – the benefits of the platform itself need to be enough.

Case 3: Banned Books Week Ain't Got Nothing on This!

Manuel is the director of a large public library in the upper Midwestern United States. His library has offered access to the Tor browser and served as a relay for several years. The library never really advertised the platform, so it has only a small, but steady, number of users. After a recent article in a major news publication discussed the "dangers of the dark web," however, the library's support of Tor was brought into greater light. A group of self-proclaimed "concerned citizens" one day approached Manuel and requested that the library remove Tor from its computers and discontinue its service as a relay. They implied that legal action could be forthcoming if the library did not follow the request and suggested that the library could be held responsible for any illegal activity on the Tor network because they serve as a Tor relay. Though Manuel remains defiant initially, he begins to question whether supporting Tor is really worth it.

How We Would Address This Issue

These types of scenarios are every librarian's worst nightmare. Just as with book challenges, opposition to the anonymous web can likely be expected if these platforms become popular/publicized enough. Unlike with "banned books," though, most librarians do not feel a strong connection to the anonymous web – yet. This may make the anonymous web seem easier to abandon if a member of the public challenges it. However, if one truly believes in the mission of anonymous web platforms like Tor, then they should support them with equal fervor as when any other information resource is challenged. Because this resource is technology-based and a bit mysterious should not change that fact.

The most important way to combat challenges to the anonymous web is through sturdy policy. Does your policy justify why access to the anonymous web is important and place reasonable limits on its use? Does the policy specifically outline procedures for when the use of the anonymous web is challenged and the role of important figures like legal counsel? By outlining these aspects before the anonymous web is adopted, you have something solid to point to as justification for organizational decisions, which takes pressure off of individual members of the library's leadership, at least temporarily. Policy further ensures that no rogue employees who agree with the protesters can deactivate access to the anonymous web without consequences – there is a clear protocol established that they would be breaking (Webster, 1972).

Situations like this one are why we suggest that any legal counsel affiliated with the library be included in the preparation stage before the anonymous web is officially adopted. It is better to assume from the start that you will face challenges rather than hope that they will never emerge. By involving legal counsel, you can feel more comfortable that your policy aligns with local and federal law and be aware of any gray areas that exist. If legal counsel is aware of the policy from the start, they will be better able to assist when a challenge does emerge. If your library does not have access to legal counsel, then there are some additional sources to consider contacting, including the Library Freedom Project (https://libraryfreedom.org/) and the authors of this book. While neither are legal experts, we have experience with the anonymous web that may prove helpful in developing a policy.

Let us say that the challenge has now happened. Members of the public are holding forums and raising hell in the media. How do you proceed? The same way that you would to a book challenge. The American Library Association's (ALA) Office of Intellectual Freedom (2021) offers a wide range of support, including guidance on how to respond to both informal and formal requests to remove resources, guidance on holding public meetings and speaking to the media, and contact information for the office. These resources are tailored toward book challenges, because that is the most common challenge to library resources but are applicable to challenges to the anonymous web as well. Additionally, agencies like the ALA itself and the American Civil Liberties Union (ACLU) could be contacted to intervene.

In fact, similar situations to Manuel's have already happened several times in the past. Readers of this book may have heard of the events at the Kilton Public Library (KPL) (New Hampshire) in 2015. The KPL became the first known public library to operate a Tor relay, during the summer 2015 (Setalvad, 2015). It was actually a group with a bit more power than just "concerned citizens" that requested the library shut down the relay: The Department of Homeland Security (DHS). Only for a very short time was the DHS's request successful. The Electronic Frontier Foundation (an organization that supports freedom on the web and is a major supporter of the Tor network), the ALA, the ACLU, and local supporters all encouraged the library board to reinstate the Tor relay. Not only did they agree, but also they allowed the relay to be upgraded to an exit relay – one of those ever-important last relays on the chain. While libraries may anticipate the possibility of challenges should they adopt the anonymous web, they should also count on those who are dedicated to the cause of privacy and freedom to provide support if these challenges do emerge. They will not be left to fend for themselves.

Some Additional Guidance on Dealing with Emerging Situations

The most important variable in how issues will progress is you! It is important not to overreact or rush to a decision. Doing so is likely to result in an improper choice. Instead, it is important to rely on communication and careful research to guide decisions. Having a clear (and relatively concise) policy in place is the best preventative measure in many situations, while having a go-to expert on the anonymous web is also beneficial to ensure any hiccups are overcome (this expert could be anyone, it just takes time and experience). None of the issues discussed in this chapter need to become an insurmountable problem. If all else fails, deleting and then reinstalling the platform will generally fix a technical issue, while open communication and support can address most political issues.

Remember that many people are simply curious about the anonymous web – just like you! So, there is no need to assume that someone asking questions about the platform is trying to challenge its legitimacy. If you can get people to chat with you about the platform, it provides a great opportunity – of course – to convert them into supporters. Like with book challenges, it may be helpful to utilize a formal process for complaints, so you know the difference between genuine interest and questioning, and legitimate complaints about the platform. Formal complaints are also simply easier to track.

It would be helpful to produce some type of manual specific to the operation of Tor within your library, particularly if you are running a relay. This will allow employees without technical experience to diagnose and address minor issues and identify when a larger issue needing immediate attention has emerged. This "manual" need not be longer than a single sheet of paper. It can list the library policy on use of the anonymous web within the library, some basic troubleshooting information (like the information you would find of the troubleshooting site mentioned in our first example case), and contact information for the individual in charge of the service. This manual may never be needed, but it does not hurt to have around!

Remember that you are not "going it alone" with the anonymous web. There are many support services out there for libraries that adopt anonymous web platforms, particularly Tor. Existing supporters of the Tor network, like the KPL, can provide a wealth of information about the experience. If you ever find yourself feeling unsure about a situation, reach out to others for advice!

References

American Library Association's (ALA) Office of Intellectual Freedom. (2021, July 23). *Challenge support*. Retrieved from https://ala.org/tools/challengesupport

Kokolakis, S. (2017), "Privacy attitudes and privacy behavior: A review of current research on the privacy paradox phenomenon", *Computers and Security*, Vol. 64: 122–134.

Setalvad, A. (2015, September 16). Libraries are banding together in support of Tor. Retrieved from https://www.theverge.com/2015/9/16/9341409/library-tor-encryption-privacy

Tor Project. (2021, July 14). Troubleshooting. Retrieved from https://tb-manual.tor-project.org/troubleshooting/

Webster, D. E. (1972), *Library policies: Analysis, formulation and use in academic institutions*, Association of College and Research Libraries' Office of Management Studies, Chicago, IL.

9   Conclusion

What Have We Learned?
What Can We Do?

We have covered a lot of ground in this book, starting with the beginning of computing itself and ending in the world of the anonymous networking and cryptocurrencies that exists today. We have covered details from the technical bases of the anonymous web, to how it may be used in libraries and information organizations, to the various potential legal and ethical concerns surrounding its use. Undoubtedly, not every question about the platform has been answered, but hopefully we have provided a solid foundation and illuminated resources by which you can investigate farther (e.g., torproject.org). We have also presented a basis upon which further research can extend our understanding of the anonymous web and those who use it.

And now we are going to say something you might not want to hear: After a half-decade, "fake news" may just be too big of an issue for libraries to really tackle. That does not mean we should not try – or that our efforts may not help to some extent – but the issues behind the misinformation phenomenon are too complex for us alone to "solve." We bring this up only so that we can contrast it with another issue, that of information privacy. No, using the anonymous web is not a perfect salve for all privacy threats out in the world, but it is about as close as any one technology can get to solving a problem. When a solution is as simple as downloading a new browser, why should not all librarians be evangelizing about it? When there are so many discussions about things we cannot easily fix, why would we ignore something that we can work on correcting. This is why we have so actively promoted the anonymous web in this book.

Always Be Skeptical/Suspicious: ABS

Using a platform like the anonymous web is a great step toward ensuring your online privacy and security. But let's say that you read this whole book and are still not convinced that the anonymous web is right for you (can we at least convince you to use a more secure browser like Brave?). Well, we do not want to leave you with nothing. Even if you have bought what we are selling, there are a few things yet that we can share to enhance your privacy

DOI: 10.4324/9781003093732-10

and security even further. This has to do with the kinds of threats that the anonymous web itself can do little to prevent, like phishing.

We propose the acronym ABS as a catchy way to remember the single most important rule when using the web: To always question anything you read. This includes traditional information literacy skills – like questioning the source of a news story – but also questioning emails you receive and offers you find online. The anonymous web can protect you from hidden threats, but not ones into which you pull yourself. For any email that includes a link to a log-in page, a file to download, or asks for information about you, ALWAYS check the full email address lines. It is very easy to edit the name that appears in the "From" line, but not to spoof a full email address. If nothing else, hit the "reply" button and check the return address that appears. The easiest thing for a scammer to do is to take a part of a legitimate email address and then use it with a Gmail or Yahoo suffix. For instance, bradylund@emporia.edu could become bradylund@yahoo.com or bradylundemporia@yahoo.com. You might say "well, that's probably just his personal account." Do not! Email the person at their trusted address (the one you have used before to communicate with them) to confirm this is the case before clicking or sharing anything. Always be skeptical.

This should also be the case any time you receive an invitation to publish in a scholarly journal. Predatory publication invitations abound in library and information science. In a period of only three months, one of the authors of this book received nearly 100 invitations to publish in what were clearly predatory journals – those that do not have a legitimate peer review process and charge exorbitant article processing charges to publish your paper (Lund and Wang, 2020). Again, it is always best to check the journal's website directly and look for clues as to whether it is a predatory publication, as opposed to clicking on any links in the email or sending your manuscript directly to the "editor."

In the research chapter of this book, we discussed the case of cryptocurrency pump-and-dumps. These schemes are also something that the anonymous web cannot prevent. It is important to be skeptical of claims about emerging technologies and trends. Is there a lot of money to make in these areas with smart investments? Sure, but knowledge of these technologies and trends is required – know what you are doing, do not just get talked into some "foolproof investment." If you can pair this skepticism skill with the technical prowess of an anonymous web platform like Tor, you are in excellent position for being Internet secure.

Our Vision for the Future of the Anonymous Web and Libraries

If we had our way, there is a vision of where we would like this book to lead – what we would like it to inspire in our readers. Our vision comes in three parts:

1 Providing access to the anonymous web in libraries.

Access includes both offering a platform like tor on the library's public computers and offering educational sessions about the platform and its responsible use. This does not mean that libraries have to provide access for ALL users or that the platform must be evangelized for users in all cases. Libraries should consider their service population, library resources, and personal beliefs to determine the extent to which the platform will be made accessible. It could be made available on all public access computers, or only a handful of computers which only adults are able to use. The anonymous web does not necessarily need to be something for which you are handing out flyers or making the computers' default browser. It should just be available in some form in every library and information organization.

2 Participation in the network.

In Chapter 5 of this book, we discuss the process of how to set up your library as a Tor network relay. Part of our vision for libraries and the anonymous web is for them to serve as relays in order to significantly strengthen the security of the network. There are some 8000 public libraries in the United States alone, another approximately 5000 each in the United Kingdom, France, and Germany. Meanwhile, there are currently only about 6000 Tor relays running in the entire world. If we manage to get one-tenth of the libraries in North America and Europe to sign-up as relays, we can double the number of relays in existence.

3 Conduct and disseminate research on the anonymous web from a library and information science perspective.

Most of the research on the anonymous web right now takes a systems and networking perspective – highly technical work that largely ignores the human element of anonymous web usage. We encourage library and information science professionals and researchers to publish their experiences with the platform as case studies, to survey users of the platform within their library, and help to improve the experience of the anonymous web from a user-centered perspective that is unique to our service-based profession. We need to stop viewing the anonymous web as a taboo and instead simply view it as another platform that patrons may use (like social media, Google Chrome, VR technology) to improve their experience and frame research in this lens rather than focus on the salacious nature of some content on the platform (a treatment that has been reserved for the dark web seemingly, even though equally horrendous content exists on Facebook, Google, and across the surface web).

It should be evident from our three aims that we are not calling for a major overhaul, but rather sensible adaptations that will help to legitimize the anonymous web and provide much-needed enhanced protections to our patrons. Libraries and librarians should not be expected to venture too far outside of their comfort zone and asking them to do so is likely to cause them to simply shut down any discussion of the anonymous web altogether. We do not want "anonymous web fan-bros," we want to normalize and legitimize the anonymous web for the purposes that it was initially designed to serve.

Final Thoughts

The "anonymous web" is a collection of platforms that hold great promise for promoting online privacy and security. Though they have been historically marked by controversy, those who endeavor to use these platforms for legal purposes have no need to fear. Rather, they will be rewarded by the anonymity a platform like Tor can provide. We implore our readers to explore these platforms for themselves, see the benefits, and determine whether it would be appropriate to share with their library's patrons. Doing so is imperative to ensuring that we fulfill our roles of promoting safe online practices.

At the end of the day, if you are reading this book, you should consider yourself very lucky. There are many places in the world today where supporting a whistleblower like Edward Snowden would be a crime, as would be talking about how to access content on the anonymous web. We can support people in these countries and ensure that our countries never regress to a similar point of oppression, by supporting the valuable anonymous web platforms we have discussed in this book.

References

Lund, B. D. and Wang, T. (2020), "An analysis of spam from predatory publications in library and information science", *Journal of Scholarly Publishing*, Vol. 52, No. 1, pp. 35–45.

The Big Glossary of the Anonymous Web and Related Topics

Welcome to the big glossary of anonymous web and related terms. Here, we include nearly one hundred terms related to the themes discussed throughout this book. The terms are organized thematically into 13 parts: principles of information rights, anatomy of the computer, networking, information systems and retrieval, code and coding, levels of the web, types of anonymous web platforms and alternatives, websites and exploration of the anonymous web, the cryptoverse, cybercrime, policy and law, literacy, and other privacy topics. This glossary is intended to provide a reference both during and after reading our book.

Principles of Information Rights

Anonymity   State in which one's identity is concealed or unknown.

Censorship   Suppression of one's right to freely communicate or exchange information with others.

Privacy   State in which someone or something is free from the observation of others. Privacy is distinct from anonymity in that, with anonymity, the product of a person's activities (e.g., a book) is known to others, but the identity of the person (e.g., the author of the book) is known only to that person or a small group of others. Conversely, if a book were kept private, then nobody would have access to it other than the author.

Security   Freedom from risk or danger; preservation of the integrity of one's data or information.

Anatomy of the Computer

Binary   Something that can hold two states; for instance, "off" and "on," "yes" and "no," or "0" and "1."

Bit   The smallest unit of information that can be communicated – a binary digit.

Boolean Logic   The branch of mathematical logic where all variables have binary options (commonly, "true" and "false").

Byte Equal (generally) to eight bits, this is the smallest unit of information that can be used to encode computer characters (e.g., letters, numbers, and symbols).

Compression A reduction in the number of bits needed to encode a message. Compression can be achieved through statistical means of reducing redundancy or removing unnecessary information.

Computer Something that performs computations; historically, this was humans, in the last century it has become a role for digital technology.

Digital Communicates using digits, such as binary data.

Packets (data) Data packaged with a set of instructions that control how the data is communicated and received. Fundamental to modern data communication on networks (such as the Internet).

Random Access Memory (RAM) A computer's short-term memory. Allows the computer to operate and retain content while the user is interacting with it.

Solid-State Drive (SSD) A computer's long-term memory. Stores data even when a computer is not in operation.

Networking

ARPANET Precursor to the modern Internet, a network designed to facilitate communication among government and research facilities.

Cookie A piece of data that "attaches" itself to a user as they navigate the web and which allows sites, advertisers, and other third-party entities to track users' behavior.

Domain Name System (DNS) A system devised to provide domain names that identify websites, associating the names that users' input with the actual IP addresses that connect sites.

Encryption Encoding of information into a representative ciphertext that can then be securely communicated across a network.

Exit Relay The final relay in a Tor path that connects to the destination user/server.

Garlic Routing Variant of onion routing, used by the I2P network, that packages encrypted messages together before sending them in order to prevent common attacks used against other networks.

Information Theory The study of how information is stored and exchanged/communicated.

Internet-of-Things A network of physical "things" that communicate with one another using the Internet in order to better perform some role. For instance, a futuristic example of Internet of Things may include a network that can detect an increase in temperature, pull your curtains, and start your air conditioner and ceiling fan.

Internet Protocol (IP) Address An identifier for every device that connects to the Internet or associated network. Analogous to how a physical home address identifies the location of a domicile (hence the name).

Internet Service Provider (ISP)   Intermediary service that facilitates the communication of data across the Internet.

Network   An interconnected collection of devices that can communicate among one another.

Network Routing Protocol   Set of data that defines rules for how other data is communicated. IP addresses are a component of the routing protocol.

Nodes   Also known as relays. Points along anonymity networks, like Tor, where information is encrypted and/or routed.

Onion Routing   Method of data communication where data is encrypted and relayed through a series of nodes in order to facilitate anonymous communication.

Routing   Method through which data is communicated among points on a network.

Traffic Analysis   Method of collecting information about data shared on networks by observing traffic patterns (how much data was sent, what frequency, etc.).

World Wide Web (WWW)   System of linked resources, stored on servers that are accessed through a public network; it is the content and organizational system that makes the Internet worthwhile for users.

Information Systems and Retrieval

Filter Bubble   A state in which search results have become so personalized based on past searching behavior that users are presented only with information that does not challenge their preconceived perceptions and biases.

Google Analytics   Analytics tracking service, operated by Google, that tracks website traffic.

Information Access   The ability to find and obtain information necessary to satisfy their needs.

Information Retrieval   The process by which information is found and obtained.

System Analysis and Design   The study and process of analyzing the functioning of a system and the needs of its users, and designing solutions to satisfy the identified needs and gaps.

Code and Coding

Compiler   Computer program that translates code inputted in one language (e.g., a human-readable language like JAVA) into another language understood by the computer (machine-readable language).

Java   Programming language developed in the mid-1990s that has gained popularity for its ease of use and broad potentials; generally used to create interactive web applications.

Machine-Readable Language   Content coded in a programming language that can be interpreted and acted upon by a computer.

Python   Programming language popular due to its simplicity and broad use potentials; also commonly used for data mining and statistical analysis.

SQL   Programming language used to manage data within system databases.

Levels of the Web

Anonymous Web   A term that is (pragmatically) synonymous with the dark web but avoids the negative connotations that have been skewed by media portrayals.

Dark Web   The "deepest" part of the web, accessible only via specialized software.

Darknet   Another term used to refer to the dark web with a decidedly negative connotation; often used when referring to illegal activities on dark web platforms.

Deep Web   The layer of the web that is hidden behind some sort of authentication screen (e.g., a log-in page).

Surface Web   The top level of the web; content that can be accessed by simply navigating to a site without requiring any log-in/authentication of the user.

Types of Anonymous Web Platforms and Alternatives

Brave   Web browser designed to optimize user privacy and block web ads while compensating content creators through the use of the Basic Attention Token (BAT), a native cryptotoken.

DuckDuckGo   A privacy-enhancing search engine that does not track and store users data and thus also mitigates issues like filter bubbles.

Firefox   Popular browser that offers elevated privacy relative to Internet Explorer and Google Chrome, but less so that anonymous web platforms.

Freenet   An anonymous web platform proposed by Ian Clarke in the late 1990s and implemented in the early 2000s that supports censorship-resistant peer-to-peer communication.

I2P   An anonymous web platform, released by the Invisible Internet Project (I2P) in the early 2000s, that is intended to facilitate private peer-to-peer communications and host eepsites: Small, used-owned sites that operate similar to blogs.

Tor   The Onion Router, the original anonymous web platform developed in the mid-1990s, was designed to facilitate anonymous communication around the world, but has evolved to allow users to access both surface website and .onion sites, unique to the Tor platform.

Websites and Exploration of the Anonymous Web

Bridges   Bridges are relays within the Tor network that are not included in a public directory of Tor relays. These relays are used to subvert efforts to shut down or block the Tor network. These bridges are used by many of the sites that exist on the network and can also be used by individual users on the network, though it does slow loading times considerably.

Eepsites   I2P's alternative to the surface websites; function like small blogs or MySpace pages where uses can upload and share content.

HTTP/HTTPS   Hypertext Transfer Protocol (HTTP) and Hypertext Transfer Protocol Secure (HTTPS) are the foundation of data communication over the Internet, serving like the "to:" statement on an email or letter. Using HTTPS, the communications sent are encrypted with Transport Layer Security that protect the communication between sender and receiver while prevent eavesdropping by third-parties.

Onion Sites   Websites that are unique to the Tor network and can only be access via the Tor browser. These sites host the "hidden services" that are discussed in relation to criminal activities on the dark web.

The Cryptoverse

Binance   Binance is one of the most popular platforms for the exchange of cryptocurrencies, with one of the largest selections of coins. The platform has received intense scrutiny from the United States, with the platform being originally headquartered in China, and then the Cayman Islands, due to a lack of regulatory compliance.

Bitcoin   The first, full-fledged cryptocurrency released for public use. Bitcoin was developed by an anonymous person/group in order to provide a decentralized, private and secure alternative to fiat currencies (those traditionally used for exchange, like the U.S. dollar or British pound. Exchange of Bitcoin is managed through a ledger system, where users compete to solve a complex puzzle in order to validate transactions, in exchange for which they receive a share of Bitcoin. This process of validation requires large amounts of energy (as the puzzles are complex and thousands of computers are competing to be the first to complete them), which is one of the major concerns with Bitcoin and similar "proof-of-work" coins.

Blockchain   A collection of cryptographic blocks, or records, that are held on a ledger and allow for information to securely be exchanged or managed without compromising the anonymity of the owner of that information. To avoid ownership of information being exchanged more than once before the ledger can be updated, transactions are validated by chaining blocks together and confirming only one transaction on the ledger. For instance, if Person A has one apple and promises to sell it to both Person B and Person C, but Person D, who is in charge of a ledger of exchanges, recognizes that the promise was made to Person B first, then Person B pays and receives for the apple and Person C neither receives nor pays for anything. This protects Person C from being sold something that does not actually exist (since the apple has already been promised to Person B).

Coinbase The most popular crypto exchange platform in the United States – essentially the Etrade of the cryptoverse. Offers over 50 popular crypto coins for trade and allows users to earn cryptocurrency in exchange for watching educational videos or "staking" their crypto: essentially, investing it back into the currency developers to help strength the currency and grow its popularity.

Cryptocurrency A digital asset managed on a blockchain ledger. Owners of a cryptocurrency actually own "keys," which are essentially passwords that validate their ownership of a certain amount of the asset on the ledger.

Dogecoin A meme-, or joke, coin developed in 2013. Dogecoin was designed as a joke and was never intended to actually have any value. However, traders, ostensibly following the praise of the coin by Elon Musk, have purchased the coin in such quantities that, in early 2021, the value of the coin peaked over seventy cents for a short period. This was a significant increase over the value of about one-half of one cent in December 2020. As of summer 2021, the price is back down to about 20 cents.

Ethereum The second-most popular cryptocurrency, after Bitcoin. Ethereum was initially released in 2015 using the same "proof-of-work" scheme used by Bitcoin; however, as of 2021, it is in the process of upgrading to "Ethereum 2.0" by transitioning to a "proof-of-stake" scheme, which validates transactions based on the consensus of those holding the large amounts of the currency. This scheme will significantly reduce the energy consumed by the network and shorten transaction speeds.

Cybercrime

Cybercriminal One who commits a crime involving the use of a computer network. Cybercrimes, like the production of ransomware and hacking of important accounts and databases, is believed to be a multi-trillion dollar "industry."

Doxing The acquisition and dissemination of previously private information about individuals or organizations. This information may be acquired through social engineering methods like phishing and shared in an attempt to shame or discredit the target's reputation.

Hacking In the literal sense, one who uses their computer acumen to overcome some obstacle in a non-traditional way. Hacking can be a completely legal act. However, hacking is often associated with criminal activities, such as hacking into a company's database through the "non-traditional" way of stealing log-in credentials of an employee.

Laundering   Investing or employing resources that have been acquired through illegal means into a legal avenue in order to "clean" it. For instance, someone who tried to deposit $1 million cash into their bank account may be met with intense scrutiny of the origins of these funds, but they would not receive the same scrutiny if they received this money in Bitcoin (especially given the anonymity of the currency) and then sold it off for $1 million over a period of several months.

Phishing   A type of social engineering – the manipulation of people into revealing private information – where targets are lured into divulging private information as the product of some scam warning or offered service to them. For instance, one may receive an email that an account of theirs has been deactivated and they must log-in immediately – using the link provided in the email – in order to recover their account. The link may lead the target to a spoofed page that looks similar to the actual website and will collect the target information when entered so that it can then be used by the phisher.

Silk Road   A defunct marketplace on the Tor network that is notorious for offering a variety of illegal or questionable items that could be purchased with cryptocurrency. Shut down by FBI in 2013 and again in 2015.

Torrents   Peer-to-peer file sharing platforms that are often used to send copyrighted or other illegal content. Most commonly associated with the program BitTorrent.

Policy and Law

Acceptable Use Policy   A policy that outlines the expected, appropriate behavior of users of a computer network. Like a "no running" sign by a pool, but much longer and full of legal jargon.

Children's Internet Protection Act (CIPA)   An act of the United States' Congress designed to protect vulnerable populations like children from accessing obscene content. This act mandates filtering of public Internet for any entity (e.g., schools and libraries) that receive discount Internet services through the government's E-rate program.

Health Insurance Portability and Assurance Act (HIPAA)   An act of the United States' Congress that prescribes the appropriate privacy and security measures that should be employed when collecting, storing, and sharing the medical information of patients.

Net Neutrality   The position that the Internet should be a neutral platform, agnostic toward what types of communications and activities are occurring on the network. This is opposed to the view that Internet Service Providers should have the capacity to prioritize certain websites or services. In this latter case, it would be feasible, for example, for an ISP to make an agreement with a retailer like Walmart to speed up access to its website while slowing access to Target, Amazon, etc.

Stop Online Piracy Act (SOPA) A failed act of the United States' Congress that was proposed in 2011 as a measure to curb online copyright infringement and trafficking of counterfeit or illegal items and services. The act would have expanded the power of law enforcement to police content uploaded to the Internet and held content aggregators (e.g., Google and YouTube) responsible for creating measures to combat all instances of piracy.

USA PATRIOT Act An act of the United States' Congress that broadened the power of law enforcement to surveil the activities of the public, particularly in their use of communications technologies like phones and the Internet.

Literacy

Data Literacy The ability to create, comprehend, and communicate data and insights that can be gleaned from that data (e.g., through statistical analysis of the data).

Metaliteracy The ability to comprehend and communicate one's own experiences and acquisition of competencies throughout the literacy learning process. It is not only about learning how to be information literate, but understanding what information literacy means and how it can be used to collaborate and improves the lives of others.

Privacy Literacy The ability to comprehend and communicate principles of online privacy and employ these principles to improve one's own privacy.

Security Literacy The ability to comprehend and communicate principles of online security and employ these principles to improve one's own security.

Other Privacy Tools

HTTPS Everywhere Available as a plug-in for many popular web browsers (and included as standard in the Tor network), HTTPS Everywhere requests that each site a user visits use Hypertext Transfer Protocol Secure, if possible, in order to further enhance the privacy of the connection with the user.

Password Manager Available as a software or plug-in for web browsers, a password manager securely stores passwords for the user, which enables the user to use more complex passwords while not worrying about forgetting/misplacing them.

Virtual Private Network (VPN) Serves as a tunnel that connects the user directly with the website/service they are trying to access, bypassing third parties that might intervene or observe their activity.

Major Websites on the Anonymous Web

Tor

Coinbase and Binance

Coinbase and Binance – the two most popular cryptocurrency exchanges – both have surface websites but are also supportive of use on the anonymous web. Coinbase provides a link directly to Tor's crypto donation site (https://donate.torproject.org/cryptocurrency/). The Tor Project accepts nine different cryptocurrencies as of summer 2021, including Bitcoin and Dogecoin (as well as Stellar Lumen, which is one of our personal favorites). The full version of Binance is not available in the United States, due to accusations of tax fraud and avoidance. However, it is possible to access the full version of Binance if you manage to hide your identity and transfer cryptocurrency that you have purchased elsewhere into a Binance account. The benefit of doing this would be that Coinbase has a relatively limited selection of cryptocurrencies and only allows you to buy and sell at a flat market rate. Binance allows you to invest in a selection of dozens of cryptos and allows for limit and stop-limit trading (allowing for you to input the value at which you would want to buy/sell rather than buying at the current rate). It more closely emulates a stock market. As with Coinbase, you can also donate directly to the Tor Project from crypto in your Binance wallet.

Okay, We Were Wrong!

In our 2019 book, *Casting Light on the Dark Web*, we advised against investment in cryptocurrency due to the volatility of the market. It is true that the market is still very volatile (and you should make major investments at your own risk), but the market proved to be stronger than we could have ever anticipated. If you had invested $100 in Bitcoin when that book was published (in late 2019), it would be worth nearly $600 today (September 2021) – and that is one of the least dramatic gains of any cryptocurrency. If you had invested $100 in Dogecoin back when that book was published, it would be worth over $10,000 today!

SciHub and Library Genesis

These platforms are very helpful to researchers... and also very illegal. The purpose of these repositories is to store millions of scholarly publications that are current published in subscription journals (i.e., circumventing copyright). Look, we cannot say that circumventing copyright is good, but the fact that this type of repository exists should highlight some issues with our current publishing models, not the least of which are the gross inequities in information access in developing countries. The charge for one article might be $19 USD, which may seem reasonable in the United States or United Kingdom, where the average academic librarian is making the equivalent of around $50000 USD a year, but very different in a country where the average librarian makes the equivalent of $2500 USD a year. So, some of the biggest users of these platforms are researchers from developing countries.

Facebook

Sure, you, reader, may be able to access Facebook on the surface web, but what about those in countries where Facebook is banned? China, the largest country in the world by population, has banned Facebook, Twitter, and other American social media as part of what is known as the "Great Firewall of China." In their place, there are Chinese-based platforms like Sina Weibo (very similar in look and feel to Twitter), but these platforms are monitored and posts censored. If you connect to the Tor network via a bridge and access Facebook's. onion site, then it is possible to connect to Facebook from within these countries where the platform is otherwise blocked. Of course, you might say "why in the world would somebody want to go that far out of their way to connect to some terrible social media platform like Facebook?" or "does Facebook do any less censoring than Sina Weibo really?"

Great Firewall of China

Censorship exists everywhere, but there are a few particularly egregious examples around the globe. They tend to overlap with the list of countries that actively attempt to block and subvert the Tor network: China, Iran, North Korea, and Cuba. China stands out because of the nation's population and GDP, as well as its rather lengthy list of blocked sites: https://en.wikipedia.org/wiki/List_of_websites_blocked_in_mainland_China. With places where information access is so restricted, we as library and information professionals should feel obligated to support a platform like Tor as a way for individuals in these countries to access information they need.

New York Times, ProPublica, BBC

For similar reasons as Facebook, many global news sources have set up. onion sites, including the New York Times in the United States and the BBC in the United Kingdom. In theory, having these. onion sites will allow those for whom their surface web counterparts are typically censored to access them. Of course, the problem is that these sites still want to make money, so content can still be hidden behind log-in screens and paywalls (in which case, readers may just turn to copies of the articles that are published on Library Genesis).

The Pirate Bay and Torrent Sites

These torrent sites are to Hollywood (and Bollywood and Nollywood) what Library Genesis and SciHub are to publishers. Most of them are available on the surface web as well, so the only "benefit" to accessing them on the anonymous web is if you have reason to believe someone would be specifically tracking what websites/downloads you are visiting/making.

Bible4u

This is a site on all major anonymous web platforms (actually, there is a version for the surface web as well – bible4u.app) that provides access to hundreds of different translations and versions of the Christian Bible. The purpose of the site is to provide access to the Bible in countries where it may be illegal or restricted to read, as well as some study guides and other information. Of course, the Bible (the Christian Bible and those of many other world religions) is available on Library Genesis as well.

I2P

I2P Forum

A lightly policed forum for the discussion of a wide array of topics. You might say it is similar to Reddit, with moderating to remove violent content. It is the most widely visited site on I2P and is probably the biggest draw of the platform.

I2P Stats

The purpose of this site is probably intuitive: It displays the usage statistics for the site. This can be useful for research purposes or just personal knowledge.

Echelon

Echelon is the developer site for I2P, so all major updates/announcements on the future of the platform are shared here.

i2p FAQ

This is the frequently asked questions page for I2P. Any basic user questions about the platform will be answered here.

I2P Wiki

Similar to the FAQ, this Wiki contains a lot of information about I2P and the features of the platform, as well as history and major sites.

Tracker2.Postman.i2p

This site is kind of a wiki of torrents. Any kind of torrent site you might be looking for can be found here. This includes the i2p equivalents of Library Genesis/SciHub for e-books and scholarly articles.

Free I2P Webhosting

Each I2P users can create their own site and it will be hosted for free on the I2P network. This is similar to the Freenet Vlogs (discussed in the following section).

Freenet

Enzo's Index and Filtered Index

Enzo's Index, established on Freenet in 2015, is the earliest index of popular websites on Freenet. It is by no means a Google or Wikipedia of the Freenet platform, but it contains more than enough resources to kickstart your browsing experience. Enzo's Index contains both innocuous sites as well as some that are potentially offensive (drug dealing, weapons, pornography, etc.). The filtered index is an alternative version of Enzo's index that has these offensive websites removed. It is probably the preferable index for most users.

Flogs

Freenet Vlogs (Flogs) are probably the main draw of the Freenet platform. They are essentially individual websites that each Freenet user can develop and use. From a visual standpoint, they look very similar to an old MySpace page, with a lot of static content – photos and text.

Freenet News

Freenet News, established in 2016, is designed to provide up-to-date news about Freenet and other anonymous web platforms and Internet privacy developments.

Freenet Message System

The Freenet Message System is one of the original features of the Freenet platform. It is the message board system for Freenet. It serves as a proto-social media platform for the Freenet network.

A Few Unquestionably Illegal Sites...
(For Entertainment and Educational Purposes)

- Dark Web Hackers: Hackers for Hire. These are real hackers who can "destroy someone's life" for a fee. They specialize in social engineering – gathering information/secrets about people by posing as someone/something they are not – spreading misinformation about a person or planting evidence of an illegal activity. If you have any sociopathic exes, you may want to be sure they are unaware of this site...
- USfakeIDs: For a measly $200 USD, you can own an official-looking driver's license from your choice of a dozen different U.S. states. Of course, this does not really help you in most cases if your records are not on file with the Department of Motor Vehicles, but it might successfully get you into a bar or club. If you have any teenager, you may want to be sure they are unaware of this site...
- Cardshop: You have heard of the "dark web scan"? I guess this is where the idea comes from. The problem is, the market does not just reveal the card holder's information on the front page of the site where anyone can find it. You have to buy the card information first. So, how the companies would be able to scan the dark web to see if your information is for-sale is beyond us... actually, not it is not. It is just complete garbage. Dark web scans are fraud.
- Peoples' Drug Store: "The Darkweb's Best Online Drug Supplier!" "Father, mother, brother, sister, all shop at peoples' drug store." "Orders ship Monday, Wednesday, and Friday. No signature is required when ordered within Canada." "We will always reship if your parcel is intercepted by customs while in transit." I mean, come on, this stuff is pretty hilarious on some level at least.
- Bit Pharma: They have got it all. 50 grams of meth for 800 euros. Or you can try your luck on a 100 generic Viagra for only 100 euros. They ship from Germany and France, so I guess they are to Europe what the Peoples' Drug Store is to Canada.
- EuroGuns: Ships to anywhere within the European Union. Of course, there is not a U.S. version of this site, because you can just walk down to your local gun store and pick any gun of your choice as easily as buying a new television.
- And, of course, there are several sites, like WeBuyBitcoins, that will purchase your Bitcoin and pay you via a PayPal account, prepaid credit card, or gift cards (you know, for money laundering purposes, ostensibly).

The thing is, even on the most hidden parts of the anonymous web, most of the content is entirely innocuous. There are "shadow blogs," which sound creepy, but they are mostly just people who like the idea of having something called a "shadow blog" and post about which political candidates favor legalizing marijuana and what their favorite brands for computer components are. They are pretty boring. There are much more worrisome things posted on surface websites like Parler than there are on most dark websites. Most dark web blogs are just kinda nerdy libertarian types who do not really try to act like "normal" people. It is the people who do try to act like normal people in their public life that should concern you if you find out they are secretly using the dark web.

The Breadth of Illegal Markets on the Anonymous Web

It is really impossible to estimate exactly how much illegal activity occurs on the anonymous web – it is a consequence of setting up a network designed to promote privacy and anonymity. However, we can look to some of the top existing illegal markets to get an idea of how many active users they have and how well federal authorities are able to police them/shut them down.

Since the shuttering of the Silk Road in 2013, traffic to illegal marketplaces has become fractured across several small markets. Three markets each have a considerable share of that traffic: Nightmare Market (yeah, that name really sets a tone), Deepsea Marketplace, and Empire Marketplace. These markets have somewhere around 50,000 combined products listed at any one time and an equal number of monthly active users. Nightmare Market alone represents over half of these products and traffic. The layout of these markets is very similar to an early Ebay. Purchases can be made using a variety of cryptocurrencies (including, of course, Bitcoin). However, buyers should beware that there is no such thing as a completely anonymous transaction when a physical product has to exchange hands.

The important number here is the number of active users of these platforms. In all appearances, it seems to be less than 100,000 monthly users. Out of context, that can seem like a lot of people, as can the 50,000 listed products. However, there are over 200 million active monthly users of Ebay and over 1 billion active listings at any time. That is just Ebay, not including Amazon, Walmart, Alibaba, or any other of these major platforms with hundreds of millions of users. Tor averages two million users per day, which also is far beyond the number of monthly users on illicit marketplaces. Legitimate users can drown out those who use the anonymous web to support illegal activities. This fact will only become more true if/as more people adopt the platform for legitimate purposes.

Web Resource Suggestions for Exploring
the Anonymous Web Further

https://torproject.org

The current iteration of the Tor project's website. It has got a slick look and markets the network simply as a secure browser. It also has an active blog and information pages – and, of course, a prominent donation tab.

https://web.archive.org/web/20071221190014/http://www.torproject.org/

Link to an earlier version of the Tor website that actually contains mention, and a whole information page about, hidden services on the network. Today, you would be hard-pressed to find any mention of hidden services, the "dark web," or the anonymous web on the modern versions of the website. The organization has seemingly done everything possible to dissociate itself with these aspects of the anonymous web and just paint it as an ultra-secure web browser (essentially, a supped-up Firefox).

https://freenetproject.org/

Current Freenet Project URL.

https://web.archive.org/web/20001017133926/https://freenetproject.org/

Very early version of the Freenet Project's website.

https://geti2p.net/en/

Current I2P web address.

https://web.archive.org/web/20041204083227/http://www.i2p.net/home

Early version of the I2P's website.

https://web.archive.org/web/20090722011820/http://www.bitcoin.org/

Earliest version of the Bitcoin website, announcing the project and how to join and earn Bitcoin.

https://web.archive.org/web/20100830025654/http://www.bitcoin.org/trade

An early directory of sites where one could buy/sell/trade Bitcoin, back when whole coins were worth no more than a couple of dollars.

https://web.archive.org/web/20130806010854/http://bitcoin.org/en/

Introduction of a more modern and sleek interface for the Bitcoin website.

https://web.archive.org/web/20140901224119/https://bitcoin.org/en/faq

An early Bitcoin Frequently Asked Questions page.

https://brave.com/new-onion-service/

Using the Tor network with the Brave browser – an introduction and how-to.

https://www.deeponionweb.com

Directory where you can find a lot of additional, current links to .onion sites.

https://blog.torproject.org/what-tor-supporter-looks-edward-snowden

Edward Snowden on supporting Tor.

https://edwardsnowden.com/docs/doc/tor-stinks-presentation.pdf

Tor Stinks! A presentation from the National Security Agency (United States) to the Five Eyes (an intelligence alliance comprised of the United States, Canada, Australia, New Zealand, and the United Kingdom) in 2007 on why intelligence agencies hate the Tor network so much. Was not intended to be declassified until 2037, but was included in the documents leaked by Edward Snowden in 2013.

https://www.huffpost.com/entry/tor-snowden_n_3610370

If you want to read the 1000-word, east-coast liberal version of this book.

Index

Access to Information and Protection of Privacy Act (Zimbabwe) 56
Advanced Research Projects Agency Network (ARPANET) 15, 16, 17, 38, 121
American Civil Liberties Union (ACLU) 114
American Library Association (ALA) 2, 7, 44, 71, 114

Berners-Lee, Tim 16, 26
BitTorrent 53, 54, 78, 126, 130, 131
Boole, George 12
Brave *see* Browsers
Breeding, Marshall 44
Bridge relay *see* TOR
Browsers 78, 111; Brave 24, 25, 26, 78–79, 85, 87, 116, 123; Chrome 77, 79, 112, 118, 123; Firefox 9, 18, 25, 29, 35, 47, 77, 78, 87, 112, 123, 134
Bundesdatenschutzgesetz (Germany) 52

Censorship 1, 3, 10, 19, 33, 50, 51, 52, 53, 54, 55, 56, 57, 58, 59, 61, 62, 70, 79, 97, 101, 103, 120, 123, 129
Chartered Institute of Library and Information Professionals (CILIP) 2
Children's Online Privacy Protection Act (COPA) 55, 126
Choose Privacy Everyday (website) 71
Chrome *see* Browsers
Clarke, Ian 31
Compression (file size) 13, 121
Cookies (computer) 23, 27, 41, 97, 121
Copyright: Law 53; Infringement 76, 126, 127
COVID-19 24, 45, 102, 111
Cryptocurrency 18, 25, 33, 77, 104, 105, 116, 117, 124, 125, 126, 128, 133

Dark web 1, 7, 10, 11, 17, 18, 19, 47, 53, 83, 92, 101, 104, 106, 112, 113, 118, 123, 132, 133, 134
Data mining 104, 123
Data Protection Act 50
Deep web 8, 9, 45, 46, 123
Dissidents 2, 17, 102
Domain Name Service (DNS) 72, 121
DuckDuckGo 24, 25, 29, 78–79, 85, 123

Eepsites 33, 103, 123, 124
Electronic Communications Protection Act 55
Electronic Frontier Foundation (EFF) 3, 114
Encryption 9, 14, 16, 26, 28, 30, 31, 33, 36, 45, 61, 89, 90, 92, 97, 108, 121; public/private keys 73
Exit relay *see* TOR

Filter bubble 79, 86
Fingerprinting (tracking) 35
Firefox *see* Browsers
Freenet 4, 17, 28, 31–32, 33, 36, 77–78, 85, 103, 123, 131–132, 134
Flog (Freenet Vlog) 131
Freesites 32

Great Firewall of China 61, 129
Google Chrome *see* Browsers
Guard relay *see* TOR

Hacker(s), Hacking 23, 24, 45, 132
Health Insurance Portability and Assurance Act 55
Hypertext Transfer Protocol Secure (HTTPS) 25, 26, 35, 36, 44, 45, 74, 79, 90, 124

International Federation of Library
  Associations (IFLA) 2
Internet 2 Project (I2P) 4, 17, 28, 32–33,
  36, 77–78, 85, 103, 123, 130–131, 134
Internet Protocol (IP) Address 22,
  72–73, 75, 76, 121
Internet Service Provider (ISP) 15, 36,
  52, 53, 57, 58, 59, 76, 112, 121

Latency 74; attacks 34
Law for a Digital Republic (France) 51
Library and Information Technology
  Association (LITA) 45
Library Freedom Project 46, 76, 114

Macrina, Alison 46
Man-in-the-middle attack 35
Middle relay *see* TOR
Mirror site 61

National Security Agency (NSA) 55
Nesting Box (analogy) 31, 34, 85, 88–89
Net neutrality 52, 126
Nigerian Cybercrimes Prohibition Act
  56
Non-exiting relay *see* TOR

Onion: descriptors 73; routing 27, 88,
  92, 104, 122; websites 19, 28, 72, 90,
  124, 130

Packets (routing) 15, 21, 34
Policy acceptable use 114, 126; internet
  use 80; privacy 42, 44, 54, 79, 94, 101,
  102
Privacy Act 54
Privacy literacy 94–95
Privacy Protection Act 55
Protection of Personal Information Act
  (South Africa) 57

Routing 17, 34, 36
Rubin, Michael 40

Service Modernization Act
  55
Shannon, Claude 12
Silk Road 10, 18, 29, 83, 126,
  133
Snowden, Edward 35, 55, 62,
  119, 134
Snowflake relay *see* TOR
Standard for Privacy (China)
  60

Telephone Consumer Protection
  Act 55
TOR: bridge 65–66, 103, 124, 129;
  browser 28, 80, 85, 92; implementation of 59, 72, 81; project 4, 9, 10, 11,
  17, 18, 19, 21, 25, 27, 29, 35–36, 46–47,
  50, 55, 70, 100, 102, 104, 111, 116, 123,
  128, 134; relay 1, 29, 72, 74–75, 76–77,
  84, 85, 110, 113, 114, 115, 118, 121; use
  of 51, 52, 53, 54, 56, 58, 59, 61, 62, 64
  79, 89–90, 101, 104
Torrent *see* BitTorrent
Traffic analysis 34, 122
Turing, Alan 12

Ulbrecht, Ross Williams 18
USA PATRIOT ACT 41, 127

Virtual Private Network (VPN)
  27, 36, 45, 70, 87, 88, 96, 127

Whistleblower 2, 9, 35, 119

Zeronet 33
Zimmer, Michael 43